Trusting God's Plan

Walking Confidently With God Through Life's Tough Seasons

Brittany Ann

EquippingGodlyWomen.com

Copyright and Disclaimers

Copyright © 2017 by Brittany Ann. All Rights Reserved.

No part of this publication may be reproduced, distributed or transmitted in any form without the written prior consent of the author. Brief quotations may be copied for the purposes of review or sharing, if and only if they are properly credited and the meaning of the quotation is not affected.

All verses are courtesy of The Holy Bible, New International Version®, NIV® Copyright © 1973, 1978, 1984, 2011 by Biblica, Inc.® Used by permission. All rights reserved worldwide. Words in brackets have been added to clarify the text without changing the meaning. All emphasis is the author's.

Disclaimer: The information included in this publication is based on the author's own opinion, experience and knowledge. Your experience may vary. No part of this publication should be construed as a guarantee, and the author will not be held liable for the use or misuse of any information contained within.

To God, who has never left my side.
To hurting women who need to know they are not forgotten.
And to my husband – none of this would have been possible without you.

Table of Contents

Introduction……………………………………………………7
Section One: Understanding God's Plan for Your Life………11
   Chapter One: Four Truths for Tough Seasons……………...12
   Chapter Two: God Is Involved……………….....................17
   Chapter Three: God Is in Control…………………………..26
   Chapter Four: God Is Good…………………………………...35
   Chapter Five: God Has a Plan……………………………...43
   Chapter Six: Why Does God Allow Tough Seasons?...........54
Section Two: Seeing God's Plan at Work in Your Life………65
   Chapter Seven: Trusting God With Your Past Mistakes…...66
   Chapter Eight: Trusting God With Your Present Circumstances…………………………………………...79
   Chapter Nine: When God Says to Wait…………………….91
   Chapter Ten: Trusting God With Your Future Plans…...…100
Section Three: Living Out God's Plan for Your Life……….110
   Chapter Eleven: Trust Is a Choice………………...............111
   Chapter Twelve: How to Trust God's Plan for Your Life...121
   Chapter Thirteen: Dealing With Doubt…………………...137
Conclusion……………………………………………………145
List of Citations……………………………………...............147
Resources……………………………………………………...148
Additional Resources…………………………………………149

Introduction

If you could ask God one question, what would it be?

Researchers conducted a poll, and the most common answer given by American adults all across the nation was: *"Why is there pain and suffering in the world?"*[1]

It's a good question. And it's one that pretty much all of us, if we were being honest, would have to admit that we wrestle with at times, even if we aren't consciously aware of it.

Sure, we sing *"You're a good, good father"* with all our hearts on Sundays and type *"Don't worry; God has it all under control! I'll be praying for you!"* when our friends post bad news on social media. But do we truly believe in God's goodness when we walk through the tough seasons in our own lives?

After all, it's not as if there's a shortage of situations in our lives that can cause even the most faithful of believers to question God's goodness and provision...

Like when you find yourself fighting with your husband more often than not. When you find out he's been watching pornography or spending money you don't have. Or when you pray and pray that your husband will be a good, godly leader for your family, only for him to turn around and make poor decisions that put your family's safety at risk. How do you trust God in that?

What about when you're forced to sit idly by as your children go through trials you'd give anything to take away? When they're bullied on the playground. When they're diagnosed with disabilities or serious health conditions. When you do your best to raise your children right, only for them to have a serious attitude problem at home and constant behavior problems at school. How do you trust God in that?

What about when you trust God with your finances, and your husband loses his job anyway? When you're already doing everything you can to stay afloat, but no one is hiring, the bills are piling up, the mortgage payment is past due, and you're just plain exhausted from the stress of it all.

What about when you find out your best friend is going through a nasty divorce, through no fault of her own, your cousin's husband has been silently abusing her for years now, and the sweet little boy on your son's soccer team was just diagnosed with brain cancer?

Where is God in all of that?

Yes, it's easy to say "God is good" on Sundays. But when the storms of life hit, that's when we begin to doubt. That's when we start to wonder *Where is God in all of this?*, *Why isn't God coming through like He said He would?*, and *Can God really use this for good, just like He promised?*

We ask ourselves *Can I really trust God though this?*, *Am I making the right choice here?*, and *So what does trusting God actually even look like anyway?*

These are the questions I'm going to answer in this book.

Of course, there are no easy answers, and I could never pretend to thoroughly understand God's heart or His plan. But when we take God at His word and really the promises He offers us through the Bible, we can walk confidently, knowing that God has everything under control, no matter how bleak our circumstances seem at the time.

This book is broken up into three sections: Understanding God's Plan for Your Life, Seeing God's Plan at Work in Your Life, and Living Out God's Plan for Your Life.

In Section One, Understanding God's Plan for Your Life, we'll dive deep into the Bible to find out what it has to say on important topics like God's sovereignty, God's goodness and God's plan. We'll answer important questions like *"Is God really in control of every single thing?"* and *"If God's really in control, why do bad things keep happening to me?"* This section contains a lot of Scripture and "head knowledge," and it's important to understand these truths to get the most out of the rest of this book.

Next, in Section Two, Seeing God's Plan at Work in Your Life, we'll look at God's plan from a more personal angle. Instead of just theorizing about what God can do in general, we'll take a look at the many ways He may be moving in your life right now. We'll answer important questions like *"Can God really use me in spite of my past?," "Does God really have a plan for the struggles I'm facing right now?,"* and *"Can I really trust God with my future?"* No matter what you're going through in this season of life or what you've been through in the past, this section should help you gain new perspective on any trials you've been facing.

Then, in Section Three, Living Out God's Plan for Your Life, we'll take a more practical look at what it means to trust God in real life. We'll answer important questions like *"What does trusting God look like?," "How do you live it out in real life?,"* and *"What are you actually supposed to **do**?"* You'll find a wealth of practical, actionable strategies here.

My prayer for you as you read this book is two-fold.

First, I hope you will find peace, purpose and perspective in the midst of whatever struggles you're facing right now. I hope you will know you are not alone and that God does have a plan for your life, even if it doesn't feel that way right now.

And secondly, I hope to challenge you and equip you to step out in radical faith, confidently taking hold of the full and abundant life God has in store for you. Because that's the kind of life God wants for you, and that's what I want for you too.

And it's all yours when you truly trust in and embrace God's plan for your life. Let me show you how.

Section One:

Understanding God's Plan for Your Life

Chapter One: Four Truths for Tough Seasons

Sarah trusted God.

Well, she *wanted* to trust God, but He wasn't making it easy.

Allll Sarah wanted in the whole wide world was a baby. Her friends had babies. Her relatives had babies. She watched them laugh and play and sing and grow. She even babysat from time to time. But it just wasn't the same.

Oh, what she wouldn't give for a tiny baby, all her own! Someone to kiss and hug and snuggle. To teach and nurture and care for.

Sarah knew she'd make a great mother too. She wasn't worried about that at all. It was as though God had *created* her to be a mother. She knew God had a special plan for her – a plan that involved her having a baby. After all, babies are a blessing from the Lord!

And yet, year after year, she waited, trying not to grow too jealous, bitter or cynical as all her friends had babies and she could not.

Where was God? Didn't He care? Had He forgotten her?

Or take Naomi, for example.

It seemed like just yesterday Naomi had everything she could have ever wanted. Not only was she happily married herself, but her sweet little baby boys were growing up so fast. It wouldn't be long until they married and had babies of their own. She could already picture the grandchildren she was sure to have soon. They'd play, sing songs, laugh... Life was full, but it was good.

Then, it all hit.

Naomi's husband couldn't provide for his family where they were living, so the family decided to move. Somewhere he would be able to find work and take good care of his family. They found a nice, new home and settled in. Started getting to know the neighbors. Making friends.

And then her husband died without any warning. Her sons did get married, but not even ten years later, they both died too. Naomi had never felt so alone.

It wasn't long until Naomi began the slippery slope into depression. Not only had she moved far away from all of her closest friends and family, but now she had just lost the three most important people in her life as well.

Where was God? Didn't He care? Had He forgotten her?

Abigail faced a different predicament. Her husband wasn't dead, but if she were being honest, she'd have to admit that sometimes she wished he was.

Grumpy, grouchy and downright mean, not only did Abigail's husband mistreat her, but he mistreated everyone around them as well. Sure, he was plenty rich, which was nice, but he was also stingy and selfish and uncaring. It hardly made it worth it. Not to mention the fact that he was always making poor choices and leaving Abigail to clean up his messes.

Abigail was smart, pretty and kind. She wasn't like her husband at all. She genuinely cared about doing the right thing. And yet, every day, she had to wake up next to *him*. Day after miserable stinkin' day. She tried to do the right thing, but it wasn't always easy.

Where was God? Didn't He care? Had He forgotten her?

Do any of these stories sound familiar to you?

Perhaps you recognize them from the Bible *(Genesis 16-18, Ruth 1, and 1 Samuel 25, respectively)* or perhaps you recognize yourself and your own story in them.

After all, these aren't isolated events. They're situations that happen to us and to those we know and love all the time.

Have you or someone you know ever:

• struggled to get pregnant?

• lost a friend or loved one?

• not known how you were going to provide for your family?

• stuck it out in a miserable relationship?

Then you know exactly what it feels like to ask yourself questions like *"Where is God?," "I thought He had a plan for me?," "Why hasn't He come through?"* and *"Doesn't He care?"*

You know exactly what it feels like to wait and wait without answers, until eventually, you start coming up with answers of your own.

Answers like, *"Well, I guess God must have just forgotten about me. I know He has a plan and all, but maybe He just forgot to include me in it. Maybe He's too busy taking care of other people with real problems. I must have just been overlooked."*

Or *"I guess that's just the way it is. Bad things have to happen to somebody, right? Sin nature and all. I guess it just happened to me. Man, I wish God could intervene, but I guess we humans just deserve what we get. Stinks to be me."*

Or *"Well, if God is all-powerful, maybe He's not so good after all, because certainly a LOVING God never could have allowed THIS."*

Sound familiar?

Yes, it's easy to tell ourselves answers like these.

And yet, when we take the time to really dive in and see what Scripture says, we see that statements like these really aren't true at all. Instead, we see the same four solid truths time and time again. They are:

1. **God is intimately involved** in every detail of our lives – not just the big stuff.

2. **God is sovereign over all things**. Not a single thing can happen unless God first allows it.

3. **God is a good, good Father** who works all things for our benefit.

4. **God has a plan**, and it's infinitely bigger and better than anything we could ever imagine.

The Bible makes it very clear: God has not abandoned us or forgotten us. We are not wandering through this world alone. Rather, God has a plan He's faithfully working out behind the scenes in our lives.

We'll unpack these four truths more fully over the next four chapters. Because when we trust God and His promises for us – it changes everything.

Let's get started.

Chapter Two: God Is Involved

An incredible 75 percent of Americans identify with a Christian religion, according to a 2015 Gallup survey[2]. Three out of every four people – that's a pretty high percentage!

So... why don't we act like it?

I mean, I don't mean to pass judgment on my fellow Americans, but all it takes is a few clicks of the TV remote, a few glances at the latest newspapers and magazines, or a few minutes listening to just about any radio station to recognize that we aren't exactly a nation known for putting God first.

Corrupt leaders are placed in positions of power. Angry mobs are rioting in the streets. Parents are hauled off to jail every day for neglecting and abusing their babies. Casual sex is pervasive. And everywhere you look, sin is glorified.

Honestly, my guess is that many, many Americans aren't actually Christians at all, but Deists – they just don't know it yet.

Deism Defined

Deism *(pronounced "Dee-ism")* is a religious philosophy that acknowledges God as the creator of the Universe, but that does not believe God is still intimately involved with the world today.

The popular analogy given is that of a clock maker who created a clock, started it in motion, and then left it alone to run all on its own.

Deists do believe that God exists, but they do not believe in miracles or divine revelation. Life simply follows the laws of nature, and everything happens because of "fate," "luck," or "chance" – not because of divine intervention.

Deism in Practice

Now of course, if you've taken the time to purchase and start reading this book, chances are you don't consider yourself a Deist. And you probably aren't one through and through. But how often do threads of Deism run through our thinking without us even realizing it?

For example:

• Did you *just happen* to be in the right place at the right time when you met your husband, or did God arrange for both of you to be there?

• Did you *just happen* to get an unexpected Christmas bonus mere days after you were wondering how you were going to afford Christmas this year? Or did God make sure you'd have everything you'd need and then some?

• Did you *just happen* to get an encouraging call or note from a long-lost friend on a day you were feeling particularly discouraged? Or was God using your friend to encourage you in a tangible way?

Sure, there probably are plenty of things that happen by coincidence, and we shouldn't go so far as to see a sign in absolutely everything. But how many times does God arrange our circumstances just how we need them only for us to completely overlook His intervention, simply because we haven't trained ourselves to recognize His handiwork?

Probably a lot more often than we realize.

The Bible on Deism

Threads of Deism may be deeply ingrained in most of us and in our culture, but there's one place you won't find them: in the Bible. In fact, the Bible is very clear: God did not simply bring His creation into existence and then leave it to run on its own; He is still intimately involved in every aspect of our lives.

Just consider these verses:

"He makes me lie down in green pastures, he leads me beside quiet waters, he refreshes my soul. He guides me along the right paths for his name's sake." – Psalm 23:2-3

It is GOD who makes us lie down in green pastures, who refreshes our souls and guides us on the right path. We are not stumbling along blindly on our own. He leads us and guides us every step of the way!

"Even though I walk through the darkest valley, I will fear no evil, for you are with me; your rod and your staff, they comfort me." – Psalm 23:4

No matter where we go, He is with us! Even in the darkest valley.

"Those who know your name trust in you, for you, Lord, have never forsaken those who seek you." – Psalm 9:10

The Lord will **never** abandon us! He's right by our side, always.

"Can a mother forget the baby at her breast and have no compassion on the child she has borne? Though she may forget, I will not forget you!" – Isaiah 49:15

As a mother myself, I know exactly what it's like to have compassion on a sick or hurting child. Even if it's three in the morning, if my child needs me, I'm there. Just TRY to pry me away from a sick baby with a bad cough and a high fever in the middle of the night. I will wind up massively sleep deprived, desperately in need of a shower, and half-crazy before I let go. She's my baby!

And God feels the same way about us. We are His children, dearly loved. He doesn't just say *"Well, good luck with that"* and let us go about our days. He's right there, taking care of us, watching over us, looking out for us. Surely you don't think we earthly mothers are better parents than God Himself, do you?

Just because you don't see or feel God at work in your life doesn't meant that He isn't. God is always at work behind the scenes, arranging circumstances as He wants them, and orchestrating events as He needs them to bring His great plan for us to fruition.

Ruth and Naomi

If you want an encouraging story about God faithfully working behind the scenes, read the story of Ruth and Naomi in the book of Ruth in the Bible.

I shared the beginning of Naomi's story in the introduction to this book, but there's more to the story.

After Naomi loses her husband and two sons, she decides to return to her hometown of Bethlehem. One of Naomi's daughters-in-law, Ruth, decides to accompany her back to Bethlehem, while Naomi's other daughter-in-law, Orpah, decides to stay behind in Moab.

With no immediate family to care for them and no way to provide for themselves financially, the two women are completely at the mercy of God to provide for them. And provide He does, though they may not have even realized it at the time.

Upon arriving in Bethlehem, Ruth goes out to gather leftover grain from the fields so she and Naomi will have something to eat. Ruth doesn't wind up in any old field, however. Unbeknownst to her, Ruth ends up gathering grain in a field owned by a relative of Naomi's, Boaz, who treats her very kindly.

Not only does Boaz make sure that Ruth is safe and provided for throughout the season, but when the season is over, he agrees to marry her.

Ruth and Boaz go on to have a son, Obed, who later becomes the father of Jesse and eventually the grandfather of King David himself – quite a family line!

Now, to the untrained eye, it may seem as though God were not involved at all. After all, Ruth simply went out to gather grain, happened to find herself in Boaz's field and he happened to marry her.

And yet, we have every reason to believe that God was involved the entire time.

What if Naomi's husband and sons had not died? The family probably would have remained in Moab instead of returning to Bethlehem.

What if Ruth had gone into a different field? She may have been mistreated, harmed, or she and Naomi may have even starved without a reliable way to provide for themselves.

What if Boaz had already found a wife or he wasn't interested? The story may have had a very different ending.

The truth is, God was working through all the events of the story to bring Ruth and Boaz together to further the ancestral line that would later include King David and eventually Jesus himself.

And all these years later, that hasn't changed. God is still hard at work behind the scenes in our lives today. Whether we believe it or not, God's workings don't depend on us or our acknowledgment of them. Even when we have no idea what God is up to or even if He's up to anything at all, He still is.

Miracles in the Mundane

I think one reason we often miss God at work in our lives is because we keep expecting that He will show up with a great pillar of fire, a flashing light, a loud boom or some other type of miracle that lets us know *"I am with you!"* And those sorts of things do happen sometimes. But when we read through the Bible, time after time we find that big, flashy miracles are usually the exception rather than the rule.

Most of the time, God prefers to work in the day-to-day. It's not that these events aren't miracles. Rather, that we're so used to seeing them that they don't seem like miracles any longer. They lose their magic, and they become all too easy to explain away.

For example:

• The future husband we pray for, and then eventually meet and marry.

• The perfect job that comes along at just the right time, or the job we're able to keep while the economy is crumbling and everyone else is losing theirs.

• The health diagnosis that alerts us to change our ways before a worse diagnosis comes along.

• The losses we encounter on a day-to-day basis that remind us to put our faith and hope in God alone.

Just because you don't see a flash of lightning and hear a loud boom from Heaven doesn't mean God isn't hard at work providing the miracle you so desperately need.

Becoming an Instrument of God's Will for Others

It's also neat to realize that just as God is working behind the scenes in your life, God is also doing the same for others. And sometimes, He even uses you to do so, often without you even realizing it. After all, when God uses day-to-day events to further His kingdom, every single one of us can easily become an agent for his Kingdom without even knowing it.

• The five dollars you donate at the grocery store check-out that answers the prayers and saves the faith of a needy family you'll never meet.

• The one, lonely neighbor you invite to church, who later goes on to lead 30 more women to the Lord as well, changing their lives and the lives of their families for generations.

• The children you raise, who will later go on to make a big difference in the world.

• The book you buy that allows your favorite Christian author to make a living doing what she loves – encouraging and equipping countless women in pursuit of Christ. *(Thank you!)*

You don't have to be called to something huge and amazing to make a difference. You just have to show up and be faithful in the little things, and then trust that God will turn those little things into big things.

One Little Yes, One Grand Plan

Honestly, if I had to choose THE most influential woman in all of Christian history, I imagine it would have to be Mary, the mother of Jesus. And what was she called to do? Have and raise a baby. That's it. It may not seem like a big job – women raise babies every day – but it was exactly what God needed her to do to accomplish His mission here on Earth, and she did it well.

In fact, the Bible is full of stories of everyday people doing everyday tasks that would play a crucial role in God's plan for humanity, even though no one knew it at the time.

Take, for example, the boy who brought the loaves and fish that Jesus used to feed the 5,000. Someone had to pack lunch that day, and I'm guessing it was the mom – just making another lunch like she did every other day. She had no way of knowing that Jesus would use her son's small lunch to perform a great miracle. She was just doing the same thing she did every day, and God used that.

Or what about the woman who prepared the room for The Last Supper? Mark 14:13-16 tells us that the meal occurred in a room that was already furnished and ready before the apostles arrived. So who furnished and prepared it?

The Bible doesn't tell us a name, but someone had to furnish, clean, and prepare the room for the most important meal in all of history. And it appears she *(I'm assuming it was a she)* did so before the apostles even arrived and before she could have had any idea how important her task would be.

For her, it would have been just another day... another load of dishes... another pile of laundry... And yet it wasn't just another day at all. She just didn't know it at the time.

No, the women in these stories likely didn't know what a huge effect their small, daily actions would have on the world, but God knew. He was working out His plan all along. And He's doing the same thing in your life as well. Even if you don't see it yet.

Chapter Three: God Is in Control

Of all the different aspects of Christianity that we could debate, God's sovereignty *(or His ultimate control and power over everything)* is one that relatively few Christians have a hard time accepting. After all, if God created the entire world and everything in it out of nothing, surely there's nothing He can't do, right?

Except when it comes to preventing the day-to-day hardships and difficulties we all face at times. That's when we start to question. Often, without even realizing it.

Except, while grappling with the tough question of "Why does God allow bad things to happen?" many Christians turn, not to God for answers, but to Adam.

After all, Romans 5:12 tells us *"Therefore, just as sin entered the world through one man, and death through sin, and in this way death came to all people, because all sinned."*

And 1 Corinthians 15:21 tells us *"For since death came through a man, the resurrection of the dead comes also through a man."*

So, in other words... it's all **Adam's** fault.

God created everything perfect. He never intended for us to worry, have our hearts broken, or endure stressful situations. But then *Adam* came along and messed everything up for all of us.

It's not *God's* fault we all endure trials from time to time. It's Adam's. And now, it's just a fact of life. Thank goodness for

Jesus who came along to fix everything Adam messed up!

Sounds like a good explanation to me.

The problem with that argument, however, is that it effectively removes God from the throne.

As though God **wanted** to help, but now He can't because His plans were thwarted by the actions of a single human.

As though a single human has power over God.

"Well," we think, *"God wanted to help. Too bad He can't. Adam messed things up. Such is life."*

The Bible on God's Sovereignty

Yet, when you look in the Bible, this isn't the picture you see at all. Verse after verse lets us know in no uncertain terms that it is **God** who is ultimately in control – not us. And that none of us – not even Adam – could mess up His plans even if we wanted to.

Just consider these verses for example:

"'Do you refuse to speak to me?' Pilate said. 'Don't you realize I have power either to free you or to crucify you?' Jesus answered, 'You would have no power over me if it were not given to you from above.'" – John 19:10-11a

Even the most powerful people on Earth have NO power,

except that which God gives them *(and could easily take away)*.

"Who can speak and have it happen if the Lord has not decreed it? Is it not from the mouth of the Most High that both calamities and good things come?" – Lamentations 3:37-38

God isn't responsible for just the good things; He's in charge of it all – good and bad.

"There is no wisdom, no insight, no plan that can succeed against the Lord." – Proverbs 21:30

What God says goes. We can't change or mess up His sovereign plans even if we want to.

These verses and countless others make it very clear that, while we do act and make decisions, NOTHING happens apart from God – whether good or bad. He is ultimately sovereign and in control over ALL.

Letting God Off the Hook

Honestly, I think the reason we are so quick to blame Adam *(or sin nature, or the Fall)*, is that we want to let God "off the hook."

We don't want to admit – to ourselves and especially to non-Christians – that a good and loving God could be responsible for allowing such horrible tragedies to happen as we see every day. We figure if we take the blame ourselves *(we are human after all)*, that it will let God off the hook, so it's not His fault and we can keep worshiping Him without hesitation.

After all, it's a lot more comfortable to be disappointed in people – especially people we don't even know – than to feel disappointment in the God we're supposed to love and trust above all else. We don't want to think of Him as less than perfect. It goes against everything we believe in!

But the fact of the matter is, we have no reason and no business trying to let God "off our hook." As the verses above make clear, God has every right and ability to do as He pleases. He does not answer to us, and He is not accountable to us.

And furthermore, when we make excuses for Him or try to explain away the parts of Him that we don't like, we are essentially saying that *our* logic and understanding are superior to His. That *we* know more than Him or are better than Him! Talk about prideful!

And not only that, but when we expect God to follow *our* beliefs on what is good and bad, we attempt to make ourselves god over God Himself.

(Let that sink in a minute... Sounds an awful lot like what happened to Satan before he was banished from Heaven. Yikes!)

Psalm 115:3 makes it perfectly clear. *"Our God is in heaven; he does whatever pleases him."*

Whether we agree or understand or not, it really doesn't matter. God is sovereign. He's the boss. He's allowed to do whatever He pleases with or without reason. He doesn't owe us an explanation.

Sometimes it's okay to simply not know, not understand or not agree. Because we're *never* going to know all of it. We're not God. We weren't meant to be. And that's okay.

The Role of Free Will

So, if God is ultimately sovereign over every single event over the course of history and there is nothing we can do to interfere with His plans, do we really have free will?

Because if we truly have free will, wouldn't that limit the power of God? Wouldn't He be limited to making the most out of whatever circumstances in life we choose for ourselves? It's a good question. And the answer lies in something called "limited free will."

Instead of full free will *(which would interfere with God's sovereignty)* or no free will at all *(which would make us little more than mindless robots)*, the Scriptures offer a third option: limited free will. Basically, limited free will says that God allows us to make our own choices, but that He gives us boundaries we cannot cross and nudges our hearts in certain situations as needed.

An analogy of this would be when I let my two young boys play in their room by themselves. I honestly don't care which toys they play with – trains, trucks, Legos or school... it's all fine with me – as long as they stay within certain boundaries. If they go outside of the boundaries I've set for them, however, then I'll intervene.

For example:

My children are allowed to play with their pretend tools – but only if they hammer quietly on the bed, not forcefully on the window. They can run and jump – but only if they are careful to avoid crashing into toys or each other.

If they start to get out of control or need help making better choices, I will nudge them in a new direction. I might poke my head in and say something like *"You haven't played with your blocks in a while. Would you like to get those out today?"* or *"I'm thinking about going outside to get the mail. Would you like to come too?"*

And I also have the power and ability to **make** them do certain things *(especially my youngest two, who I can still literally pick up and move)*, but I only use it when needed. Usually, I just let them make their own decisions as long as they remain within my predetermined boundaries and guidelines.

And I imagine it's the same way with us and God.

As long as our actions fall within certain predetermined boundaries and guidelines, we are generally allowed to move and act as we please. He gives us free rein and free will. But God always maintains "veto power" if we get out of control or if He needs us to do or not do a specific action to bring about His ultimate plan.

God's Revealed Will Vs. God's Sovereign Will

In *The Case for Faith* by one of my favorite authors, Lee Strobel, Strobel arrives at essentially the same conclusion by differentiating between God's revealed will and His sovereign will.

Strobel defines God's revealed will as the set of commandments and guidelines God has revealed to us, either through the Scriptures or through other sources such as nature, education or the church. God's revealed will includes things like the 10 commandments *(Exodus 20:1-17)* or the fruits of the spirit *(Galatians 5:22-23)*. And while He would certainly never prefer it, God does allow us to go against His revealed will, and all of us do, all the time.

Strobel defines God's sovereign will, on the other hand, as God's overarching master plan and purpose for our lives and the lives of all people throughout the history of creation. God never lets us go against His sovereign plan, even if that means essentially forcing us to make a certain decision over another one when needed.

We can find examples of this all throughout the Bible:

• Exodus 9:12 tells us the Lord hardened Pharaoh's heart.

• Exodus 12:36 tells us the Lord later made the Egyptians favorably disposed toward the Israelites.

• In Genesis 20:6, we read that the Lord kept Abimelek from sinning against Abraham's wife, Sarah.

• In Acts 16:6-7, we learn that the Holy Spirit prevented Paul from preaching in certain areas of Asia.

And there's no reason to believe that the God who caused and prevented events in the Bible times isn't still orchestrating events the same way today.

Thankfully, that's a truth we can take great comfort in.

Taking Comfort in God's Sovereignty

Yes, it's easy to get angry at God when we see great injustice in the world or when things don't go our way. It's easy to scream *"Not fair!"*

But, on the flip side, how many injustices *haven't* occurred and how many things *haven't* gone wrong because God was right there, guiding everything every step of the way? How many tragedies has God already saved us from that we have NO idea?

I think of the time my husband and I were driving in another state with our young children in the back. We were turning through an intersection when another car, driving at an excessive speed, suddenly appeared out of *nowhere* and just *barely* missed hitting us. I have no idea how we all didn't end up in the ER that day. Only God.

Or I think of the time that my husband and I accidentally fell asleep while watching our oldest – who was just a toddler at the time – at a friend's lake house. I woke up suddenly, didn't see him in his pack-n-play next to me, and immediately panicked.

The house was still under construction. He could have climbed up the stairs and fallen from the unfinished second floor. He could have wandered out into the water – and he didn't know how to swim. He could have taken off down the street and been abducted for all I knew.

So I did what any mother would do – I immediately jumped up and started searching for him with incredible speed, worried about where he might be or what sort of trouble he might have gotten himself into. He's a good boy, but he was only two, and we were in a strange house with plenty of dangers I didn't know if he knew to avoid.

Thankfully, it took me less than a minute to find him. He was sitting happily out on the back deck, eating a strawberry yogurt, watching the boats glide by on a beautiful, calm summer morning. I don't think I've ever hugged him so big as I did that morning.

Yes, I have encountered hurts and trials that I don't know why God allowed. I have no idea why God allows famine and cancer and abuse. But man, am I thankful for the many tragedies He has spared us from – often without me even knowing!

Chapter Four: God Is Good

So, I'm not the most trusting person by nature.

Sure, I do believe that most people are basically good and want to help others when they can, but I also believe that there are limits to their goodness. Ask too much or push too far and you're likely to be disappointed – often, without warning.

As a result, I've learned to rely on myself. I don't open up easily, I don't depend on others for things I can provide myself, and I **don't** ask for help. I've learned along the way that I'm the only person who will never leave me, let me down or embarrass me, and therefore the only one I can really trust.

Even with my own husband, who has shown me time after time that he is here and truly cares, I'd really rather just do things myself than rely too heavily on him.

I'm getting better. But I definitely have a way to go.

As unfortunate as this is, however, what is even more unfortunate is that this is the exact same attitude many people take with God.

"Sure, He's pretty good," they think. *"But I don't know if I can really trust Him. It's probably just a matter of time until He lets me down. After all, He has a whole world to run. I highly doubt He has **my** best interests in mind. Yes, He's been good to me in the past, but who's to say that that won't change tomorrow?"*

Or worse yet, many people will go so far as to actively mistrust God. They assume that He's a big jerk in the sky who rules with an iron fist and is just looking for any excuse to punish those who don't toe the line.

They see all the hurt in the world and imagine He's up there, playing with people's emotions, causing hurt after hurt after heartbreak, without taking so much as a second to show compassion on or even consider the plight of us mortals down here who are just trying to get along.

Have you ever felt that way at times?

The good news is, nothing could be further from the truth!

God is absolutely CRAZY about us and is SO good to us. He loves us even when we don't deserve it, and He's not going anywhere. And when we truly understand that, it changes everything.

God's Great Love for Us

You don't have to dig very deep into the Bible to find a wealth of verses about God's great love for us. From Genesis to Revelation, the Bible is full of verses that explicitly and implicitly tell of God's great love for us.

John 3:16 – arguably one of the most popular verses in the entire Bible states His love simply:

*"**For God so loved the world** that he gave his one and only Son, that whoever believes in him shall not perish but have eternal life."*

Now, if that's not love, I don't know what is! Forget flowers and chocolate. God sacrificed His one and only son – for us!

One of the prayers I pray most frequently is simply that God will keep my children safe. Whether it's inclement weather, terrorists, burglars, killer bees... I just want my children to be safe and happy and healthy.

And yet, when given the choice between keeping His own son safe or providing for us – God chose us.

Can you even imagine??

Say tomorrow you were on a boat, it started to sink, and you could only pull one person into the boat with you. Everyone on the boat would be saved, but everyone else would drown. Would you reach for your child, desperately gasping for breath, head barely bobbing in and out of the water? Or would you reach for the known terrorist – the one who *caused the boat to sink in the first place* - calmly treading water next to him?

I know who I'd reach for. I wouldn't even have to think about it.

Or what if you were in a shopping mall during an earthquake and you could only help one person out before you were all smashed to pieces? Would you grab your child and run like the dickens? Or would you leave your child behind to die a slow and painful death, his cries ringing in your ears, while you helped a known and unrepentant sex offender out the door at the very last moment?

To every mother, the answer is obvious. You help your child! That's your *child*. It doesn't matter one bit if your kid was throwing a temper tantrum five minutes earlier. That's your baby and you would do absolutely **anything** for him – especially if his life were on the line. It's not even a question.

And yet, that's not what God did.

While we were still sinners – while we were intent on doing wrong and turning our backs on God – He gave up His one and only son for US.

God loves you SO much that He won't let *anything* get in the way of His love for you. And that's the truth.

God's Love for Us Isn't Based on What We've Done

Every once in a while, I'll get an email from a lovely lady who is struggling spiritually because she doesn't feel worthy of God's love. These letters always make me sad, both because I've been there so I totally know what it feels like and because it simply isn't in line with what the Bible says at all.

Friend, if you feel that you have to "measure up" to earn God's love for you – let me tell you right now, that is a lie straight from the pit of Hell designed to distract you, disable you and keep you from the full and abundant life God has for you. There's just no other way to put it.

Nowhere in the Bible does it say *"Sally Smith was a super good Christian, so God loved her extra much. Too bad you don't measure up."*

In fact, quite the opposite! Romans 5:8 says, *"But God demonstrates his own love for us in this: While we were still sinners, Christ died for us."*

Jesus didn't die for us because we measured up. Jesus died for us because we COULDN'T measure up.

And if you look throughout the Bible, you'll see the same story time and time again. God's people made huge mistakes. They had serious character flaws and committed massive sins. God would come through in a miraculous way, and not even two pages later, they'd be doubting and sinning again.

And yet He loved them and took compassion on them anyway. Just like He does for us today.

Take these famous Bible characters, for example:

• King David committed adultery, murdered the husband to cover it up, lied about it, and then added the woman to his many wives.

• Moses killed a man, didn't follow God's directions, and then was prohibited from entering the Promised Land.

• Abraham lied about his wife, took a second wife, and tried to bring about God's plan His own way.

• Rahab was a prostitute and a traitor to her country.

• Before Paul became an apostle, he harassed, persecuted and murdered Christians.

• The apostle Peter denied Jesus three times – and he was an apostle!

Or take me for example. I got pregnant out of wedlock, while attending a private Christian university, and had to drop out for a while after it came out in a public and very embarrassing way. I'm not very good at respecting my husband, I yell at my kids more often than I should, and I still have trouble trusting God and His promises all the time.

I know what God wants me to do. I hear Him plainly. I've seen miracles both big and small more often than I could possibly count. And yet, I still struggle to listen and obey.

And I'm definitely not alone in this. Romans 3:23 tells us, *"for **all** have sinned and fall short of the glory of God."*

We all make mistakes. We all fall short. We all mess up. But God continues to love us anyway. Because God's love for us is not based on what we do, but on who He is and who we are in Him.

Again, consider your children as an example. When your children were first born, they were literally incapable of doing *anything* to earn your love. They couldn't talk, or do any cool tricks or buy you flowers for Mother's Day. They couldn't say "Thank you" or "I love you" or "You're doing a great job." They didn't even know what those things mean.

As infants, your babies were selfish. They needed to be fed and changed and rocked around the clock. They never stopped to think about you or your needs. They just took and took and took, and then they broke your stuff.

If it has been a while since you were in the baby stage, maybe you don't remember. I don't know. But my littlest one is just over a year now, so I still remember clearly. *(Or at least as clearly as I can now that I have three!)* Parenting a newborn is exhausting, thankless work!

How many days have I spent walking around like a zombie, desperately needing a shower and something more nutritious to eat than whatever scraps I managed to grab while making them all lunch? I have no idea. I can barely remember how old I am some days *(not even joking here)*, much less all the many, many thankless things I've done for my kids.

And yet, I don't love them *less* for it – I love them *more*! Because they are my babies and I would do absolutely anything for them. They are my babies, and I am their mama. They need me. Especially the littlest ones. They literally depend on me for their very survival. Their entire future will depend in very large part on the decisions I make right now in the day to day.

And will I let them down? No! Not if I can help it. They're my babies.

And how much more so will God – who is perfect, who is knowledgeable, and who has every resource at His disposal – love and care for us?

I may not be the perfect parent. Or the perfect spouse. Or the perfect Christian. In fact, I can assure you that I'm not. But thank the Lord I serve the One who is.

God Will Take Care of Us

The good news is, the same God who is crazy in love with us is the same God who will always make sure that we are provided for. Sure, it may not always be in the way that we hope, but it will always be in our best interests.

Just consider these verses for example:

"So do not worry, saying, 'What shall we eat?' or 'What shall we drink?' or 'What shall we wear?' ... But seek first his kingdom and his righteousness, and all these things will be given to you as well." --Matthew 6:31,33

When we set our hearts on following God, we don't have to worry about the rest. He will take care of it!

"This is the confidence we have in approaching God: that if we ask anything according to his will, he hears us. And if we know that he hears us—whatever we ask—we know that we have what we asked of him." – 1 John 5:14-15

God not only hears our requests – He promises to grant them when they are in line with His will. That's powerful! And what is God's will for us? Well, we can find that in Jeremiah 29:11:

"'For I know the plans I have for you,' declares the Lord, 'plans to prosper you and not to harm you, plans to give you hope and a future.'"

Friend, if you are questioning God's love for you today, let me assure you: God is CRAZY about you! He loves you with an everlasting love that will never ever go away. Not because of anything you've done or haven't done, but because of who He is and who's you are.

Rest in that today.

Chapter Five: God Has a Plan

It was just after 6 a.m. on a Tuesday, and I was lying in bed, trying to sneak in a few more moments of rest before a busy day. It was my middle child's third birthday, and the boys were excitedly playing with birthday balloons in their room, waiting for their baby sister to wake up so we could open presents.

I heard peals of giggles... then a thud... then a scream. Within seconds, my oldest son was at my doorway, a worried expression on his face, looking for help.

Quickly making my way to the boys' room, I picked up my younger son, thinking he had just fallen *(as little boys are known to do)*, only to realize a minute later that his mouth was full of blood and it was coming out quickly.

I yelled for my husband as I tried to figure out where the blood was coming from, how serious the injury was, and how to make it stop. There was blood on the towel, on his clothes, on mine... and every time I tried to take a peak, more blood just kept right on coming.

It took a few minutes, but I did eventually get both the blood and the tears to stop. I checked out the damage below – a deep cut right in the middle of his bottom lip.

It looked fairly serious, but not life threatening. So with just over an hour to go until the emergency care clinic opened down the street, we decided to open presents to keep the birthday boy happy and occupied while we waited to take him in.

At the emergency care clinic, the nurse didn't look too terribly concerned.

*"It **could** heal fine on its own,"* she explained. *"Or we could give him a single stitch just to make sure it heals correctly. We won't give him any medicine first, so it will hurt, but it should go pretty quick and easy, and the stitch will fall out on its own once his lip heals... It's up to you."*

A difficult decision! I definitely didn't want to put my son through any pain – *especially on his birthday* – but I didn't want his lip to heal funny either.

I decided to go ahead and get him the stitch, just in case.

Five minutes later, I was holding one very scared little boy down on the table as still as I could while the nurse readied the needle.

Why Does God Allow Tough Seasons?

So, why am I telling you about the time my middle child got a stitch in his lip?

Because so many times in life we find ourselves right there on that table, in the midst of a tough season, wondering how a loving God could possibly allow bad things to happen to us.

"This hurts!" we protest. *"This isn't fair!"* we complain. *"Where **are** you?"* we demand. And *"Why don't you **DO** something??"* we insist.

After all, surely a God who loves us, who can keep us from harm, would *want* to keep us from harm, right?

And yet, what if life's tough seasons aren't punishments, but blessings in disguise? What if all the hardships and stresses we face aren't just a result of God looking the other way, but the result of God doing what's best for us, even if we don't understand it at the time?

To my three-year-old, getting that stitch was torture! He screamed and kicked and thrashed about as I did my very best to hold him still on the table. It was without a doubt the worst pain he has ever known.

And instead of mommy protecting him and keeping him safe, here I was, holding him down on an uncomfortable bed in a strange office room so some scary nurse could stick a needle through his lip.

He didn't have the words to express himself at the time, but I wouldn't be surprised if he was feeling the same way. *"Why would you? How **could** you??"*

He hated it. He didn't understand. It was torture.

And yet, I *did* understand, and I had to make the choice that was best for him in the long run, even if it was painful at the time.

God Has a Plan

I share this story to story to illustrate a point: When we face trials and hardships in this life, it isn't the result of God being mean or not caring about what happens to us. Instead, oftentimes, we go through tough times in this life because God DOES care and does want what's best for us – He simply has a different perspective than our own.

You see, when I look at my life, I can only process information through the lens of what I already know.

I know what has happened in my life thus far. I know some stories from other people's lives, some stories from history, and some information about how things typically work. I have some ideas of what I'd like the future to look like. But I don't know the whole story. I can't see the whole picture.

It's like looking at one tiny fraction of a painting, seeing an ugly brown color and declaring entire painting ugly. After all, everything you see really isn't that attractive.

And yet, if you could unveil the rest of the painting, you would see all of the gorgeous reds, yellows and greens and realize the painting is actually a breathtakingly beautiful fall scene. You only see one small piece of the muddy river flowing across the bottom. You don't see the vibrant colors of the leaves on the trees, the wispy blue clouds floating lazily across the sky, or the small children laughing and running on the muddy river banks.

And unfortunately for us, that's the way it's always going to be on this side of Heaven.

We look at life and we only see the tiniest sliver. We don't see our entire lives, or the lives of those around us. We only see our very limited perspective on the events in our lives that we've experienced and noticed.

But God sees it all. And He sees His grand purpose behind it.

The poor choices your children have been making lately? You feel like a failure as a mother. You worry that you aren't doing enough, that you aren't involved enough, or that your children are going to head down the wrong path in life.

But God sees something entirely different. Where you see

"failure," God sees "faithful." And He's using you to plant seeds in your children's lives so when they are ready to turn to Him, they'll know just where to find Him. You've been pointing the way all along.

The financial struggles you've been dealing with lately? You worry about making ends meet and still having anything left over at the end of the month. You'd like to give generously, but you just don't see how it's possible. You wonder if God will ever come through for you, and if so – *when?*

But God sees something entirely different. He sees the discontent and jealousy you feel when others have nice things you can't afford. He sees the worry you feel when you don't trust Him to take care of you. And God would rather you endure those financial struggles now, knowing that your faith will be so much stronger because of it, than give you all the money your heart desires that you don't really need.

The fighting you and your husband have been going through lately? You see a marriage in trouble, but God sees something entirely different. God sees all the potential areas of conflict that are keeping you and your husband from truly joining together as one, and He's bringing them out into the open now so you can deal with them and grow closer than ever before. You aren't a failure, and you aren't messing everything up. God is simply using this tough season to prepare you for amazing things to come.

And while it can be difficult to know what God is up to or what plan He has for our lives, we can have full confidence that He does have one, even if we don't see it or if it doesn't make sense to us at the time.

Isaiah 55:9 reminds us, *"As the heavens are higher than the earth, so are my ways higher than your ways and my thoughts than your thoughts."*

We don't understand it all. We're not supposed to understand it all. Sometimes we simply have to trust that God knows what He is doing and let that be enough.

When We Don't See the Whole Picture

It isn't just our tough seasons that make trusting God's plan for our lives so difficult. It's the fact that we're left in the dark, wondering what God has up His sleeves, if anything at all.

When we're five minutes late for work, we don't see that terrible car crash we would have gotten in if we had been on time that day.

When we struggle year after year with our financial situation, we don't see the trouble our children would have gotten in if we had had the money to put them in those extracurricular activities they begged to join but we couldn't afford.

When our children walk away from the faith, we don't see how the Lord is still working on them and through them to bring them – and several of their new friends – back to Him someday.

We simply don't know. And it's aggravating. BUT – it's also a good thing.

Because, honestly, would you *want* to serve a God who could be fully understood by mere mortals? Who could be placed all neat and tidy into a human-sized box? I wouldn't.

No, the God I serve is too big for that. His ways are higher than our ways and His mind infinitely more powerful and intelligent than we could ever imagine. So, no, we'll never understand it all.

And besides, if we *could* see God's entire plan, all laid out, we'd be overwhelmed.

Could you imagine God coming up to you tomorrow and saying *"Hey there! I need you to lead 1,394 people to me, save 30 starving children from orphanages and find homes for 50 homeless families right here in your city. But don't worry. You've got 30 years."* You'd be overwhelmed! You wouldn't know where to start!

But what if God said, *"Hey, I need you to go talk to that mom sitting by herself over there. Just talk to her. Find out her story."* Now **that** you could do and watch God's grand story unfold from there.

God's Plan is for More than Just Us

Another thing we need to keep in mind: God's plan is not all about us; it's about all humanity. And while we are each infinitely important to God, at the end of the day, we are each only one person.

So if God has a plan that involves suffering for one but benefits 99 others, isn't that right and just? Even if that person is you? Even if you don't see how it will help 99 others yet?

Just because you don't know why God allows you to go through tough times doesn't mean that there isn't a reason.

The truth is, we may never know how God can use our current trials and hardships to help those around us, either currently or in the future – not on this side of Heaven, anyway. We simply have to trust that whatever His plan is, He has everyone's best interests in mind.

Does God Cause Bad Things to Happen or Only Allow Them to Happen?

I was only in fourth grade when I heard a great analogy that stuck with me to this day.

A friend told me, "God doesn't **cause** bad things to happen; He just allows them. Like when you're teaching your kids to ride a bike. Sure, sometimes they'll fall... and you'll be right there to catch them. But God doesn't *push* us off the bike."

Made sense to me.

Unfortunately, however, as nice of an analogy as it is, it simply isn't true. Sometimes God DOES push us off the bike. Sometimes God doesn't just catch us when we fall. He's the one who pushed us off in the first place.

Consider Isaiah 45:7, which says:

"I form the light and create darkness,

I bring prosperity and create disaster;

I, the Lord, do all these things."

And Isaiah 53:10a, which says: *"Yet it was the Lord's will to crush him and cause him to suffer"*

Or what about 1 Samuel 1:6, which says that God closed Hannah's womb? Or Exodus 9:12, which says that God hardened Pharaoh's heart? Second Thessalonians 2:11 says that God will send the lawless man a "powerful delusion so that they will believe the lie," and 2 Corinthians 12:7 says Paul was given a thorn in his flesh, a messenger of Satan.

Surely, a loving God would never do something like *that*... would He?

Well, yes, He would. God does intentionally cause us harm.

But before you mutter, *"I thought this chick was a Christian! Guess not...."* and throw this book across the room, keep in mind: God does cause us harm, BUT He never harms us just to harm us, as though He delights in our suffering. Of course not! Instead, God will sometimes use a lesser harm to help protect us or others from a greater harm or to bring about His perfect plan for our lives, even if we don't appreciate it at the time.

Take Joseph in the Old Testament, for example. His brothers sold him into slavery and told their father he was dead, all because they were jealous. That's pretty bad!

Yet in Genesis 50:20, Joseph tells his brothers, *"You intended to harm me, but God intended it for good to accomplish what is now being done, the saving of many lives."*

God not only allowed Joseph to be sold into slavery, He intended for it to happen! All because God had a plan for Joseph and his family that was far greater than the momentary trials Joseph would have to endure for God to bring His plan to fruition.

And it's important to remember: Joseph didn't know what God was up to when he was left in the well or sold into slavery. He didn't know God's plan when he sat in prison, seemingly forgotten, after Pharaoh's wife wrongly accused him of coming on to her. Surely Joseph felt abandoned and forgotten, sitting there all alone.

But while Joseph didn't know, God did. God had a plan all along. Just like He does for us.

Going back to the bicycle example, we could say, *"Yes, God would push us off the bike... if we were headed into oncoming traffic and didn't know how to stop. Getting a scraped knee would be painful, but it would be a whole lot less painful than getting run over. And it would motivate us to learn how to avoid the situation in the future."*

Similarly, God could cause your husband to lose his job, through no fault of his own, if that job loss would give him the time to prepare for and the motivation to apply for an even better position opening soon – a position he wouldn't have even noticed if he were still employed at his old job.

And God could allow your child to be bullied at school – if that bullying was the catalyst you needed to teach your child who she is in Christ and to look to God in all things – not to the world. Yes, you and your child would be angry and upset while the bullying was happening, but you would both be stronger as a result of it. It would be worth it.

God's Plan and Our Responsibility

There's one thing I want to make very clear, however. The fact that God can use all our decisions for good does NOT take away our personal responsibility to do the right thing. In other words, we can't say, *"Well, it's okay for me to sin because God can ultimately use it for good."*

While God can ultimately use all our decisions for good, His ability to do good does not take away our responsibility to right. God has given us rules and boundaries for a reason, and He still expects us to obey Him. And according to Matthew 12:36, Romans 14:12, 2 Corinthians 5:10 and 1 Peter 2:4, each of us will be held accountable on judgment day for the choices that we've made throughout our lives.

Furthermore, when you do make a wrong choice, you cannot say *"Well, how do I know God didn't cause me to sin, if He does that sometimes?"* The Bible makes it very clear: each and every one of us will be held responsible for the choices that we make.

James 1:13-14 tells us, *"When tempted, no one should say, 'God is tempting me.' For God cannot be tempted by evil, nor does he tempt anyone; but each person is tempted when they are dragged away by their own evil desire and enticed."*

God isn't going to take a sinless, upright Christian who is genuinely trying to do their best and force them to sin. Rather, He takes those people who *chose* to sin and He uses their sins to help accomplish His purposes.

The truth is, God has an amazing master plan He is working out behind the scenes and all of us will play some role in it, whether we like it or not. The only question is – what role will you play? Will you work with God to further His plan for all of creation, or will He have to carry it out in spite of you? The choice is (mostly) up to you.

Chapter Six: Why Does God Allow Tough Seasons?

In the last chapter, we talked about God's plan in general. In this chapter, I want to get more specific. Why *specifically* does God allow us to go through tough seasons in our lives? How does it help His plan *practically*? What does it actually help accomplish?

Before I get into that, however, there is one thing we have to keep in mind.

Suffering is a Part of Having Free Will

While the idea of living in a world without any suffering sure sounds nice, the truth is that it doesn't work that way. As long as we have free will, we have the capacity to choose, and that includes the capacity to choose evil and suffering. And the fact is, we will.

Remember: when God originally created the Garden of Eden, it was perfect. There was no suffering. God did not create suffering, and suffering was not a part of God's original design. God simply created the *possibility* of suffering when He created us with free will.

So Adam and Eve made choices every day, and eventually, they made a bad choice. And each of us – even if we were given a completely clean slate – would eventually make those same wrong choices too.

Don't believe me? Just consider how many times you have

sinned since you first came to faith in Jesus. You were washed clean and clear. And yet, you still return to sin and suffering time and time again. It's a part of having free will. Adam and Eve found a way to sin, despite having no sin nature, and you would too.

How God Uses Pain and Suffering for Our Benefit

Just because some degree of suffering is inevitable doesn't mean that the difficult times we go through have to be all negative, however. The good news is that no matter what type of stresses or hardships we face in this life, God can and does work in them and through them for our good, even if we don't see it at the time.

Here are five ways He does this:

1. God Uses Tough Times to Draw Us Closer to Himself

While no one particularly enjoys going through a time of stress or hardship, it's hard to deny how powerful times like these can be in terms of calling us closer to God.

As Timothy Keller writes in *Walking with God through Pain and Suffering*, "You don't really know Jesus is all you need until Jesus is all you have."

And while there is always a distinct possibility that these same struggles and hardships could potentially lead us away from God into a period of doubt and despair instead, it is on the other side of this doubt and despair that we emerge stronger, more faithful and more confident in the hope we believe.

And honestly, it makes perfect sense. When times are good, we get distracted. We get so busy chasing other interests and worrying about things of this world that we forget all about the God who has so graciously provided us with so many blessings to begin with.

After all, when was the last time you hit your knees in fervent prayer to thank God for all of the many, many blessings He has given you in this life? I don't know about you, but I'm not sure I've ever done that. Yes, I do thank God regularly and genuinely for all He has given me and my family. But if I'm hitting my knees in fervent prayer and really calling out to God with all I have, it's because some type of tragedy is involved or I fear one will come my way soon.

In 2 Corinthians 1:8b-9, Paul writes, *"We were under great pressure, far beyond our ability to endure, so that we despaired of life itself. Indeed, we felt we had received the sentence of death.* **But this happened that we might not rely on ourselves but on God**, *who raises the dead."*

If anyone knew what it was like to undergo suffering for the sake of the Gospel, it was Paul. Beaten, stoned, shipwrecked, imprisoned, robbed, exposed to death multiple times, attacked on every side by Jews, Gentiles and demons alike... Paul experienced it all. And yet, it only served to strengthen His commitment to the cause of Christ.

In fact, in 2 Corinthians 12:10, Paul tells us exactly how he felt about all of the suffering he endured for the gospel, and I can pretty much guarantee you it's not how the majority of us respond to even the mild pain and suffering we endure today.

He writes, *"That is why, for Christ's sake,* **I delight in weaknesses, in insults, in hardships, in persecutions, in**

***difficulties.** For when I am weak, then I am strong."*

Paul knew suffering, but he knew His Lord as well, and that was enough for him. Just imagine what type of impact it would have on our faith and our relationship with our Creator if we took that same stance today.

2. God Uses Tough Times to Draw Us Closer to Each Other

Yes, Jesus may be all we need, but having close friends and family to walk alongside us can really help our faith journey as well. And that's one of the reasons why God allows tough seasons: to draw us closer – not only to Him – but also to each other.

Ecclesiastes 4:12 tells us, *"Though one may be overpowered, two can defend themselves. A cord of three strands is not quickly broken."*

Whether you're suffering an attack on your health, an attack on your marriage or an attack on your faith, times of trial and testing are always much easier to endure with good, godly friends on your side who can encourage you and keep you pointed in the right direction.

And yet, how many times do we keep our true struggles and hardships to ourselves in a prideful effort to make our lives look better than they really are?

Do your closest friends know the full extent of the hidden things you struggle with? Do you know their deepest, darkest fears, worries and struggles as well? Or are you hiding behind a wall, thinking you're protecting yourself, when all you're really doing is creating a distance between you and the loved ones you need the most?

I personally know a girl who was abused for years, and although I knew her at the time, I had **no** idea. She always seemed happy, outgoing and confident to me. It was only after things became worse that the truth came out and she was able to escape a truly awful situation.

Sure, God could have prevented the abuse. She could have continued in that relationship. But by allowing things to get as bad as they did, she was able to find freedom from that relationship and to exchange it for much closer relationships with godly friends and family instead.

Who knows just how many families and friendships have been healed as a result of tragedies that threaten to take everything away? Honestly, sometimes we need those reminders – as unpleasant as they may be – to help focus our attention right back where it needs to be.

3. God Uses Tough Times to Warn Us of Potential Danger

I once heard a story of a man who was paralyzed from the waist down and who had no feeling in his legs at all. And while the absence of pain may seem like a positive, his inability to feel pain actually put him in danger.

You see, if he were to place a hot cup of coffee on his lap without thinking about it, there would be no pain to warn him to move the cup before he badly burned himself. And if he were ever bitten by a poisonous snake or spider, he likely wouldn't know to go to the emergency room until it was too late.

In this way, pain isn't just a hardship we have to endure as we pass through this life. It's a warning sign God uses to keep us from stumbling into danger or to prompt us to flee the dangerous situations we've already gotten ourselves into. We just don't always know it at the time.

• The scary medical diagnosis that motivates you to improve your health before things get worse...

• Marriage troubles that motivate you to take action to improve your marriage before it's too late...

• The pile of bills that forces you to sit down and create a budget instead of simply letting money fly out the window without another thought...

Yes, tough times can be the result of poor choices we've made. But they can also be gifts from God, given to us just when we need them in order to help us grow, choose a better path or learn a valuable life lesson.

In fact, Psalm 78:34 tells us the following about the Israelites: *"Whenever God slew them, they would seek him; they eagerly turned to him again."*

It's just like when your children disobey and you have to discipline them. No loving parent **enjoys** disciplining their children. It's not fun for anyone. But it is sometimes necessary, because sometimes discipline is the only way they will listen and obey. And sometimes a little discipline is exactly what we need to bring us back in line with God's will for our lives once again as well.

4. God Uses Tough Times to Help Us Mature Spiritually

One of God's primary goals for us here on Earth is to make us more Christ-like, and as Christians, that should be our ultimate goal as well. After all, if we really, truly believe God is who He says He is and that He will accomplish what He says He will accomplish, then there is nothing more we should want in this life than to be more like Him.

But the question remains – How do we actually **do** this? What steps do we need to take, practically speaking, to help us grow in faith and reach a higher level of spiritual maturity?

James 1:2-4 gives as a clue: *"Consider it pure joy, my brothers and sisters, whenever you face trials of many kinds, because you know that the testing of your faith produces perseverance. Let perseverance finish its work so that you may be mature and complete, not lacking anything."*

Yes, spiritual disciplines like prayer, Bible study and fasting are one way to grow in spiritual maturity. But it is also during the rough seasons of life that we develop perseverance and ultimately spiritual maturity in Christ as well.

I've seen this to be true in my life, and I imagine you have too. And we are not alone in this.

In fact, when I asked *"What is the one thing that has really helped you grow in your faith in the past?"* as a part of the 2016 Equipping Godly Women reader survey, two answers came up time and time again: *"Depending on God in tough times"* and *"Seeing prayers answered."* These responses confirm what we all fear to be true – that God wants to grow us, and sometimes He uses the tough times in our lives to do just that.

Yes, it hurts at the time. But when you consider how much

good can happen both in our lives and in the lives of others as the direct result of the tough situations that we are dealing with now, we really can have true *joy* in our sufferings, just as James instructs us to above.

5. God Allows Us to Go Through Tough Times So We Can Help Others Through Their Tough Times

One reason our seasons of hardship and trial can be so difficult to understand is because, sometimes, our suffering may not even be about us at all. Rather, sometimes God calls us to endure troubles now so that someone else may be healed or strengthened in their troubles later.

Just look at 2 Corinthians 1:4. It reads, *"[God] comforts us in all our troubles,* **so that we can comfort those in any trouble with the comfort we ourselves receive from God."*

Yes, God *could* erase all suffering and heal all wounds. He has the power to do that. He spoke the universe into existence; He could speak pain and suffering out of existence too. But in His infinite wisdom and goodness, He decided that wasn't the best course of action to take. Instead, He chooses time and time again to use us – His people – as agents of healing and restoration for each other.

And what better way to minister to those around us who are hurting than to come alongside them as someone who has experienced the same sorrows and worries as well?

You see, it's one thing to quote some Scripture and say, *"It's going to be alright. The Bible says so."* It's quite another to be able to walk alongside someone through their hurt and to be able to say *"You're going to be okay. I've been here before. God got me through it, and He will get you through it as well. I'm here for you. I understand."*

So what struggles have you been through? And how can you use them to minister to those who are in the exact same situations today? The truth is, you have knowledge and insight and compassion that others who haven't been through that same situation simply don't have.

Sometimes people will send me emails, asking for advice. They want to know how they should respond to an adult child living in sin or to toxic family members who are threatening the health and relationships within their family. And honestly, I don't know. Sure, I can look up some principles in the Bible and do some research online, but I'm never going to have the depth of insight and compassion that someone who has been in those exact situations would have.

That's why, if you've been through situations like these or others – that's not necessarily a punishment – it could a gift! After all, God doesn't steal life's blessings away from us for no reason. Instead, He constantly gives us both blessing and hardships to prepare us and equip us with the exact strengths, skills, knowledge and disposition we need to carry out whatever plan He has for us to accomplish someday.

I think about the ways God has used both the good and the bad circumstances in my life to make me just the person He needs me to be to accomplish His plan for me, and I am continually amazed. Looking back, it's crazy to see how He is working good things, bad things, big things, little things – ALL things – for His glory and His plan.

You may not see it now. You may not ever see it at all. But God has a plan. We just have to trust it.

Happiness is a Privilege, Not a Right

I think part of the problem we have with the idea of pain and suffering is that we see a happy life as the default option, and anything less as something "bad" or "less than." As though we are entitled to a perfect, worry-free life and anything else is a rip-off.

But honestly – whoever promised us that we would have a life full of happiness, sunshine, rainbows and nothing else? That's certainly not what the Bible has to say. In fact, John 16:33 tells us plainly, *"...In this world you will have trouble..."*

Jesus himself endured mocking, beating, betrayal, hunger, tiredness, the death of friends and family and so much more. What makes us think that we should somehow be immune?

The truth is, all of us began this life as sinners who deserved nothing at all, except for maybe death. Romans 6:23 tells us *"For the wages of sin is death..."* and in John 15:5, Jesus reminds us *"apart from me you can do nothing."* God is in no way required to give us life itself, much less a great one.

And yet – He does! All of us – every single one of us – have SO much to be thankful for. Why aren't we glorifying God in that? Why are we so busy dwelling in the negative that we completely miss all the many, many blessings God showers on us every single day?

When is the last time you truly, from the bottom of your heart, thanked God for the fact you woke up this morning, for the clothes on your back or for the roof over your head? Have you thanked God for your ability to read and write, the fact that you don't live in a war-torn country, or the fact that you can read Christian living books like this one without the fear of persecution and beheading for your entire family?

When is the last time you thanked God that your mother lived through childbirth, that you still have your eyesight, or that you have enough money in your possession to have a bank account, even if there isn't as much money in it as you might like? Have you thanked God for toilets that flush or the clean drinking water that's available with the push of a handle? What about the fact that your children can go to school and receive a good education?

You're pretty lucky, you know. Most Christians throughout the world don't have it nearly as good as you do.

Please understand, I am not trying to make light of any difficult situations you may be going through currently. I know it hurts.

But just because you are dealing with a stressful or worrisome situation right now does not mean that God isn't there for you. He's still right there by you, working out His plan, taking care of everything behind the scenes, and showering you with more goodness and blessing than you'll ever know – even if it doesn't feel like it at the time.

Section Two:

Seeing God's Plan at Work in Your Life

Chapter Seven: Trusting God With Your Past Mistakes

If you had the opportunity to change anything in your past, would you? Would you rectify mistakes and start over fresh? Or are you happy with everything in your past just the way it is?

It's a tricky question, and honestly, I'm not sure how I would answer it personally. While I'm very happy with where I am in life right now, that hasn't always been the case.

You see, I spent a lot of years being ashamed of my past. Convinced that if anyone knew everything I had been through and done, they wouldn't like me. That they would reject me, and I'd be all alone.

So I hid. I kept relationships shallow. I moved a lot. Stuck to big, anonymous churches where I could blend in and remain invisible. Shared only the best parts of myself while hiding the rest.

Even with my own husband, I've always struggled to open up and let him know everything I'm feeling and everything that's going on. Not because he has ever given me any reason not to trust him – he hasn't. I just prefer to keep people at a distance. Feels safer that way.

Compared to the Biblical giants we discussed earlier in chapter four, my past is really nothing to write home about. I haven't murdered anyone or committed adultery, like King David. I haven't persecuted Christians like Paul or been a prostitute like Rahab. I've never denounced Jesus publicly, like Peter. I wasn't responsible for the fall of mankind like Adam and Eve.

No, compared to many characters we read about in the Bible, I'm doing pretty well.

And yet, you don't have to do much or go through much for Satan to have ammo to use against you.

For me, it was the fact that I was depressed throughout most of middle school, high school and college. And it wasn't being depressed that bothered me – I have no problem with that. It was the way people looked at me and treated me because of it. No one meant any harm, but I saw how they pitied me, saw me as "less," and didn't think I'd ever amount to much.

And then there was the fact that I got pregnant out of wedlock while attending a private Christian university. That was fun. I remember sitting silently in class while another girl *(who was married)* shared with the class that – Surprise! She was pregnant! Everyone gathered around, talking all at once, so excited for her. *When was she due? Was it a boy or a girl? Wasn't she so excited???*

They even had cupcakes. *(Yes, it was totally the cupcakes that did me in.)*

Because there I sat, silently, in my shame. With a baby quietly growing in my belly too, but no cupcakes for me. Because no one was excited about my baby. *My* baby wasn't a cause for celebration. *My* baby was cause for a quiet dismissal from school.

Actually, I didn't know if they'd kick me out or not, but I sure didn't want to find out. So I hid my growing belly for as long as I could and then dropped out of school before they had the chance, completely abandoning the degree I was only one semester away from completing.

For several years after that, I wondered if I had messed everything up. If God had had this great, amazing plan in store – just for me – but now I couldn't take part in it because I had disqualified myself.

I'd go to church and hear all the AMAZING things the mission teams were doing overseas. *I* wanted to do amazing things. *I* wanted to make a difference. *I* wanted to change the world. But I couldn't. I was stuck at home with a baby, and it was all my fault.

I had made a mistake, and it was a big one. I knew better than to have sex outside of marriage. I knew it was wrong. But I did it anyway, and I ruined everything.

Or so I feared.

Your Failings are Not a Hindrance to God

There was just one problem with my line of thinking. If I – as a mere human – could have derailed God's plans for me *that* easily – just by making one wrong choice – wouldn't that contradict God's sovereignty?

After all, as we discussed in chapter four, the Bible makes it very clear that God is sovereign over all things. He is in total control over absolutely every situation and has the final say over absolutely every decision that is made. Including my getting pregnant.

So that means – I *couldn't* have messed up His plan. He must have planned for it all along. If my getting pregnant would have "messed up" God's plan, He could have (and would have) prevented it, the same way He hardened Pharaoh's heart in Exodus 9:12 and kept Abimelek from sinning against Abraham's wife Sarah in Genesis 20:6.

Now please understand, I am **not** saying that God necessarily **wanted** me to have sex and get pregnant. After all, sex outside of marriage is a sin, and James 1:13b makes it clear that *"...God cannot be tempted by evil, nor does he tempt anyone."*

But long before my now-husband and I even met, God knew that we would choose sex before marriage. And, long before my now-husband and I ever met, He took that choice into account. It was part of His plan all along.

God's Had a Plan All Along

You see, God doesn't plan our lives by waiting until we are already halfway through them and then saying *"Okay, let's see what she left me to work with... Well, shoot. That's not really what I had in mind. Guess I'll have to think of something else. On to Plan B."*

Rather, He has a master plan He's been working out since the dawn of creation, and He assigns each of us a certain, specific role to play in it, taking into account what type of people we will be and what decisions we will make.

Take Judas for example *(You can read the story in Luke 22, if you aren't familiar with it)*. Surely God wouldn't have **wanted** Judas to betray Jesus. God wills that all would come to Him in perfect fellowship. But since God knew in advance what Judas would do, He was able to work Judas's actions right into His perfect plan, so that even when Judas made a terrible mistake and Satan thought he had won, the kingdom of God was still advanced in a very powerful way.

Judas may have committed one of the worst sins imaginable, but there's no sin so great that God can't overcome. God redeemed Judas's sinful actions for the glory of God, and He still does the same for us today.

It took several years, a few insightful sermons, a few faithful whispers from God and a few glimpses of the future He has in store for me, but I no longer worry about having messed up God's plan for my life. I'm confident that I'm right where He wants me to be and that He's going to use me right where I am. He already is.

Sure, I may have abandoned my teaching degree and I may not be able to pack up and head overseas to help war-torn, third-world countries, but that was never God's plan for me. He had something else in mind the entire time. Something I can do right here, from home, on my couch, with the kiddos napping in the next room.

God's plan for me wasn't for me to teach 30 elementary school children how to read and write, but to teach hundreds of thousands of women how to love the Lord, follow closely in His footsteps, and teach their children to do the same. I'm still a teacher – just not in the capacity I had imagined.

And God's plan for me also wasn't for me to head overseas for a short-term mission trip or two. As fun as that would be, and as much as I'd like to go someday, God's call for me is to be a full-time missionary right here from home.

Sure, maybe there are things I can no longer do due to the decisions I've made, but I don't feel like I'm missing out. Instead, I know God allowed a few good things to be removed from my life so that there would be time and space for the even better plan He was already busy crafting behind the scenes.

And I have a very good feeling that was God's plan all along.

Satan – the Great Accuser

So now you know some of my backstory. What about your own? Have you ever wrestled with guilt and shame over choices you've made in the past? Have you ever wondered if you've let God down or somehow disqualified yourself from the full and abundant life God originally had in store for you?

Have you ever stopped to consider where those feelings of guilt and shame come from?

After all, men and women were not created to feel shame. It simply was not a part of God's plan for us. Genesis 2:25 tells us: *"Adam and his wife were both naked, and they felt no shame."*

Yes, Adam and Eve were both buck naked with no shame and not a care in the world. I don't know about you, but I certainly have **no** desire to run around with all my nakedness hanging out. *No thank you.* But Adam and Eve? They had no shame and nothing to hide.

Until that changes in the very next chapter.

The New Living Translation translates Genesis 3:7 this way: *"At that moment their eyes were opened, and **they suddenly felt shame** at their nakedness. So they sewed fig leaves together to cover themselves."*

So... what changed?

The simple answer is they ate the apple. But that's not all.

At the very moment they took that first bite, Adam and Eve also severed their perfect relationship with God. They tarnished their soul with the dark, black stain of sin. And they gave the devil a foothold, or a "grasping on point," where he could grab hold of their lives and their thoughts and influence them for evil. Satan did it to them way back then. And he still does it to us today.

You see, Satan isn't just the "bad guy" in a children's book. He is a real being with a real vendetta against Christians and Christianity, and he will attack us in absolutely any way he can.

That's why 2 Corinthians warns us that Satan schemes and tries to outwit us and 1 Peter 5:8 instructs us to: *"Be alert and of sober mind. Your enemy the devil prowls around like a roaring lion looking for someone to devour."* Because he really is out there, and he really is trying to destroy and incapacitate us.

And it isn't just the "big sins" Satan tries to tempt us with, either. After all, getting someone to commit murder probably isn't very easy. *(Don't believe me? Go ask your spouse to help you kill someone. Chances are, he won't be on board.)* And not only that, but it's unnecessary.

Satan doesn't have to make us into horrible, evil sinners. He just has to disarm us or distract us so we're effectively worthless for the cause of Christ. And one very real way he does this is through shame.

In fact, in Revelation 12:10, Satan is referred to as "the accuser of our brothers and sisters." Because that's exactly what he does – he accuses.

First, he tempts us with a variety of very appealing-looking sins until we eventually take the bait. Then, he flips the switch and tells us how horrible we are and how we should be so ashamed of ourselves for what we have done.

When's the last time you thought *"I'll never be good enough," "I've messed everything up,"* or *"I have nothing special to offer?"* Sound familiar? Yeah, I've been there too. We all have. The lies Satan whispers to us are far from original. We ALL hear them from time to time.

But the good news is, when we look at Scripture to see the truth of what God says about us, we can recognize these lies from Satan for what they really are, and we can choose to believe the truth instead.

Truths like:

- We are children of God *(John 1:12, 1 John 3:1)*

- We are chosen, holy and dearly loved *(Colossians 3:12, 1 Peter 2:9)*

- We are created in God's own image *(Genesis 1:27)*

- We are a new creation *(2 Corinthians 5:17)*

- We are God's friends *(John 15:15)*

- We are God's workmanship *(Ephesians 2:10)*

- We are more than conquerors *(Romans 8:37)*

- We are citizens of Heaven *(Philippians 3:20)*

These are the truths we can rightfully cling to.

How God Sees Us Despite Our Sins

So if thoughts like *"I'll never be good enough"* and *"I have nothing special to offer"* are lies that we all tell ourselves from time to time – why do we still believe them?

I believe one thing that makes Satan's lies so convincing is that they always contain a small grain of truth. Yes, we have all messed up and fallen short *(Romans 3:23)*. No, we're not "good enough" all on our own.

But the good news is, we don't have to be! God doesn't expect us to be perfect, and neither should we. After all, if we could achieve perfection all on our own, then we'd have no need for Jesus, and his death would be in vain.

No, the Bible makes it clear that we cannot earn our salvation by being "good enough." It's only through accepting his death and resurrection and the forgiveness He offers that we can ever be forgiven and made clean.

And how God delights in forgiving us and making us clean, pure, spotless and wholly loved once again, no matter what it is we have done in the past! When God looks at Christians in good standing with Him, He doesn't see our past sins, mistakes and failures. He sees His perfect Bride, dearly loved.

Just consider these verses, for example:

Hebrews 8:12 tells us, *"For I will forgive their wickedness and will remember their sins no more."*

Micah 7:18b tells us, *"You do not stay angry forever, but **delight** to show mercy."*

Romans 5:1 tells us, *"Therefore, since we have been justified* *through faith, **we have peace with God** through our Lord Jesus Christ."*

This doesn't mean God is ignorant or forgetful, of course. He still knows everything.

But what it does mean is that, in Christ, we don't have to be trapped under the weight of guilt and shame any longer. We can call Satan the liar he is and walk in full confidence and freedom, knowing that we have been forgiven and redeemed.

Galatians 5:1a says, *"It is for freedom that Christ has set us free."*

Friend, no matter what has happened in your past, God has a plan for you. And it's better than anything you could ever hope or imagine. It's time to break free from Satan's lies and from the bondage and shame of your past so you can begin walking in true freedom today.

Here's how.

How to Find Freedom from Past Sin and Shame

1. Confess Your Sins

If you are a Christian with sin in your life that you have yet to ask forgiveness for, you should feel some degree of guilt or shame. It is this guilt and shame that compels us to turn to God and seek forgiveness.

So start with confession, or admitting your wrongdoings. Be honest with yourself and own up to whatever it is you have done or failed to do. Confess your sins to God first *(He already knows about them anyway)*, and then to whomever your sins have hurt, as well as a fellow sister-in-Christ who can help hold you accountable.

Sin and shame thrive in secrecy. Don't give them the chance. Get everything out in the open where you can remove it properly.

2. Repent

Next, once you have admitted your sin, you need to repent, which basically means to feel sorrow and regret, and to do a 180 and head in the opposite direction. It's not enough to simply admit your sins and feel bad about them. You have to actually stop doing them, even if it's hard.

3. Seek Freedom from Bondage

Of course, not all sins are easy to break, especially in cases of addiction. This is because, when we allow sin to enter our lives, we give Satan a foothold or a "grasping on point," from which he can influence and control our lives, and he isn't going to let it go of it easily. Therefore, if you have sins that are keeping you in spiritual bondage, stronger measures may be needed.

Two of the absolute best resources I know of on spiritual strongholds are the books *The Steps to Freedom in Christ* and

The Bondage Breaker, both by Neil T. Anderson. I went through both books and *The Steps to Freedom in Christ study guide* in high school, and it absolutely began a period of great healing and transformation in my life. I know it can for you too.

If you have sins you struggle to break free from, I would strongly encourage you to check out one or both books. But don't stop there. Speak to your pastor, a strong Christian mentor or a trusted godly friend. Speak to a professional counselor or doctor, if you need to. Do whatever it takes to find true freedom once and for all. Yes, it is hard, but **it is worth it**.

4. Forgive Yourself

If God, who is perfect, pure and holy, can forgive you – so can you. You are not allowed to hold yourself to a higher standard than God does *(as though you were a more righteous judge)*, and you don't want to say that Jesus's blood is insufficient for your sins *(it's not)*. When God declares you forgiven, you are forgiven. Period. End of story.

5. Walk in Truth

Of course, changing your outlook and your actions going forward isn't always easy. That's why you must commit to walking in truth.

What sins do you struggle to avoid? What Scriptural truths do you struggle to believe? Find relevant Scripture, write it down, memorize it, and refer to it constantly. Meditate on it day and night until it becomes a part of you and you start living according to it.

Are you struggling with guilt and shame over your past? Memorize Romans 8:1, which says, *"Therefore, there is now **no condemnation** for those who are in Christ Jesus."* Repeat it to yourself every time those feelings creep back in again. Say it out loud if you need to. Write it on your hand if you need to. Spray paint it on your walls if you need to *(yes, seriously)*. Do whatever it takes for you to be able to proclaim God's truth victoriously.

6. Surround Yourself with Positive People

And lastly, be sure to surround yourself with positive people who see and bring out the best in you. Honestly, this was a very crucial step in my own healing process. It wasn't until I emptied my life of pretty much everyone and everything that I was not only able to root out all the bad stuff, but really grow in all the good stuff as well.

Yes, this is very difficult to do. As hard as it is to break free from friends who are toxic, it can be harder still to sever relationships with others who really are good people. But coming from someone who gave up every single friendship I had prior to this point of healing – it was worth it. Yes, sometimes I miss some of my old friends – they were wonderful people who did nothing wrong – but it was what I had to do to find healing, and I'm so glad I did.

Chapter Eight: Trusting God With Your Present Circumstances

So in the last chapter, we talked about how we can trust God and walk with God in right standing, even if our past is marred by poor choices and shameful situations of our own doing.

But what if you haven't made any huge mistakes in your past, and yet you're still struggling under the weight of a burden you didn't ask to bear?

After all, it's one thing to deal with the consequences of your own poor choices. It's quite another to find yourself in the midst of trying circumstances through no apparent fault of your own.

Perhaps you or someone you love is struggling with chronic health issues. You'd love to embrace the full and abundant life God has for you, but simply making it through the day is struggle enough. Between the pain and fatigue that lay you up for hours or even days at a time, the frequent doctor's appointments and the constant medications, it's almost more than you can handle. How do you trust God in that?

Or perhaps you feel trapped in a loveless marriage, and you're not sure what to do about it, or if you should do anything at all. You know God hates divorce and you don't like the thought of it either, but the thought of staying is quickly becoming almost too much to bear.

Plus, you worry about your children. Surely all the constant fighting can't be good for them. You've never been so miserable or felt so alone in your life. How do you trust God in that?

Or maybe you're struggling financially, and it's really putting a strain on your faith. You know you're supposed to tithe and give generously to those in need, and you want to, but how *can* you when you're barely making ends meet? You know God promises to *"...meet all your needs according to the riches of his glory in Christ Jesus" (Philippians 4:19)*, but you haven't seen it in your life. How do you trust God in that?

Finding Peace in Romans 8:28

The good news is that for every difficult circumstance we face, the Bible is full of encouraging Scripture verses we can cling to in order to help see us through. Verses like Romans 8:28, which reads, *"And we know that in all things God works for the good of those who love him, who have been called according to his purpose."*

One thing we must be careful of, however, is that we always have to read the verses for what they actually say – not just what it appears they say on the surface.

Romans 8:28 is sweet, encouraging and incredibly popular, but it's much more than just a sweet-sounding promise of provision – it gives us quite a bit of direction for our lives as well. So let's break it down further and see what it **really** says.

• *"And **we know**..."* There is no uncertainty in this verse. There is no "maybe." As Christians, **we know** that God works all things together for good. We don't have to question. We can have full confidence in this!

• *"...that in **all things**..."* Not just the good times, but the times of tragedy too. Whether we understand God's will or not. Even when we don't know what He's up to, God ultimately works **all things** together for our good.

- *"...that **in** all things..."* Of course, just because God can use all things *for* good doesn't mean that everything that happens *is* good in and of itself. Cancer is not good. Divorce is not good. Abuse is not good. Infertility is not good. But God can work **in** and through all these burdens to bring out the goodness that He desires. The goodness comes from the sum of all the parts – not from every individual part itself.

- *"...**God works** for the good..."* Furthermore, this working takes time. So if you don't understand how your circumstances can possibly be good right now – that's okay! The verse doesn't say that God instantaneously turns our suffering into rejoicing. Instead it says *"**God works** for the good."* It's a work in progress. Give it some time.

- *"...God works **for the good**..."* It's also important to keep in mind that God's version of "good" and our version of "good" may not always line up. As humans, we tend to prioritize whatever makes us happier, more comfortable or further ahead financially. God, however, places a far greater value on making us holier and furthering His will here on Earth. Your present circumstances may not be fun or comfortable, but if they are making you more Christ-like and furthering God's plan – that's ultimately a good thing.

- *"...of **those who love him**..."* Unfortunately for non-Christians, this verse only applies to Christians in good standing with the Lord. Those who have not entered into a loving relationship with God cannot claim this promise. Yes, God does love everyone in the sense that He wants everyone to have a loving relationship with Him, but if you have chosen to turn your back on God and remain in a state of sin or separation from Him, you shouldn't expect to receive His full blessing for your choices.

- *"...who have been called **according to his purpose**."* Again, God's ultimate goal isn't to make us happy and comfortable. It's to set His perfect plan into motion in our lives. And as we discussed in chapter three, God is able to do whatever He needs to in order to make sure His plan comes to fruition, even if we don't particularly enjoy it at the time.

In other words, if you have turned your back on God and have refused to accept the many blessings He so freely wants to give you, then don't be surprised when things don't go your way. You've rejected God and His plan for you, you've gone outside your hedge of protection, and now you may have consequences for that.

But if you are a Christian who is fully committed to walking with Jesus and growing in faith every day, you can have **full** confidence that God really does have your best interests in mind, even if you don't understand how He's working everything together just yet.

Esther and Mordecai

Want an inspiring and encouraging story about how God works everything together for our good – even when we don't realize it at the time? You can find exactly that in the Old Testament book of Esther.

The story begins in chapter one at a grand banquet in the palace of King Xerxes and his wife, Queen Vashti. What starts off as a grand party quickly turns sour, however, as Queen Vashti refuses to appear for the king and his party guests, and he promptly removes her as the queen.

With King Xerxes suddenly in need of a new queen, orders go out that beautiful young virgins from every providence in the realm are to be brought in for a chance to become the next queen. The girls are given a year's worth of beauty treatments and the finest foods in preparation for their one night with the king.

One of the women – a lovely young Jewish woman named Esther – stands out among the rest, and she is ultimately chosen to become the new queen.

Unfortunately, however, Esther's life isn't the fairy tale you might expect. After her cousin, Mordecai, refuses to bow before the king's favored official, Haman, Haman asks the king to issue a decree calling for the destruction of all Jewish people within the land. And the king agrees, not knowing Esther's Jewish background.

It is at this point that Esther is forced to make a terrifying and potentially life-altering decision. If she goes before the king without first being summoned, he could very easily put her to death for her boldness. If she doesn't, however, her entire race could be wiped out. The clock is ticking, and she must act fast.

So in Esther 4:14, what is easily the most recognized verse of the book, Mordecai pleads with Esther, *"For if you remain silent at this time, relief and deliverance for the Jews will arise from another place... And who knows but that **you have come to your royal position for such a time as this?**"*

The interesting thing about the book of Esther is that it is one of only two books in the Bible where God's name isn't mentioned at all. *(The other is Song of Songs.)* And yet, it's not hard to see His hand at work behind the scenes, guiding Esther to the exact place she needs to be so He can use her to save God's people from certain destruction.

At least, it's not hard for us to see anyway. We have the benefit of reading the whole story from start to finish from an outsider's perspective. We can skip to the last page of the book to see how it all turns out. But have you ever stopped to consider what it must have been like for Esther as she was going through these circumstances?

You see, being chosen as the queen likely wasn't the fairy tale dream come true we make it out to be. In fact, if you focus on the details of the story, Esther's life is riddled with pain and suffering. For example:

• First, Esther loses both her mother and father when she is young.

• Then, she is taken away from her friends and family to enter the king's harem. While this may sound romantic or exciting, Esther likely had no choice in this. This probably wasn't a beauty contest she voluntarily tried out for. She may have essentially been abducted against her will.

• Say goodbye to any dreams Esther may have had for her future, including any potential suitors she may have had her eye on or the possibility of starting a loving little family of her own someday. As queen, she wouldn't have been the king's adored and devoted other half. She would have been little more than a favored concubine – one of many. She wasn't even allowed to approach the king unless he summoned her first, much less have a real, loving relationship with him.

• Plus, not only does Mordecai put his own life at stake when he refuses to bow down before Haman, but he puts the lives of the entire Jewish population at stake as well. The proclamation is signed. The war against the Jews is happening and is irreversible.

• And more than seventy-five thousand people died as a direct result of the actions that were taken throughout the book, most of whom had done nothing wrong.

No, if you look at any of the individual events of the book, the situation looks pretty grim. From start to finish, the entire book is full of tragedy after tragedy, especially considering that no one at the time would have known what God was up to or if He was even concerned about them at all.

They didn't have the Holy Spirit or the Bible like we do today. They couldn't skip forward to the end of the book to see how everything would turn out. They just had to trust God and hang in there as best they could. They had to tell themselves the stories of their faithful ancestors and hope and pray that God would take care of them too.

And isn't that what it's like for us today? We can't skip the parts we don't like or peek forward to the end of the book to see how it all turns out. We may never understand God's plan for our life on this side of Heaven. We just have to cling to God's promises and remind ourselves of the times He's been faithful before.

Except now we also have the added benefit of the Holy Spirit and the reassurance of the Bible to help carry us through.

Bible Stories About God's Provision

Are you going through a tough time right now? A time where you find yourself asking *"Where is God?" "Does He still care?"* or *"Will He come through?"*

If so, the good news is that even if you don't see what God is up to in your life right now, the Bible is full of verses and stories that can encourage and strengthen you no matter what circumstances you're facing today.

After all, no matter how alone you may feel or how much you may feel like no one else understands, chances are someone in the Bible has been through the exact same thing or something very similar. And just as God saw them through their tough situations, He will see you through too.

For example:

• Do you have friends or family who are mistreating you? Read the story of Joseph in Genesis 37, 39-50 to see how God remained faithful in Joseph's life despite his many, many trials.

• Are you grieving the untimely loss of a loved one? Read the story of Job to inspire you to walk in faith and trust the Lord, even when there are no easy answers.

• Are you struggling to trust God with your finances? Read the story of the Widow of Zarephath in 1 Kings 17:7-24 to see how God turned what little she had into an abundance, in direct proportion to her faith.

Bible Verses About God's Goodness

Would you prefer an encouraging Scripture verse you can write down, memorize, or hang up somewhere where you will see it often instead? The Bible is full of those too. Here are a few of my favorites:

"The Lord himself goes before you and will be with you; he will never leave you nor forsake you. Do not be afraid; do not be discouraged." – Deuteronomy 31:8

"The Lord is my light and my salvation—

whom shall I fear?

The Lord is the stronghold of my life—

of whom shall I be afraid?"

--Psalm 27:1

"The righteous person may have many troubles, but the Lord delivers him from them all." – Psalm 34:19

"God is our refuge and strength,

an ever-present help in trouble.

Therefore we will not fear, though the earth give way

and the mountains fall into the heart of the sea,

though its waters roar and foam

and the mountains quake with their surging."

--Psalm 43:1-3

"But he said to me, 'My grace is sufficient for you, for my power is made perfect in weakness. Therefore I will boast all the more gladly about my weaknesses, so that Christ's power may rest on me.'" – 2 Corinthians 12:9

"And the God of all grace, who called you to his eternal glory *in Christ, after you have suffered a little while, will himself restore you and make you strong, firm and steadfast."* – 1 Peter 5:10

Whatever it is you're going through today, take heart. Someone in the Bible has been through it before. God saw them through it, and He'll see you through as well.

Jesus Understands What You're Going Through

Not only can we take comfort from the stories of the Bible characters who have gone before, but we can also take comfort from the fact that Jesus himself has been right where we're at and knows exactly what we're going through.

After all, God didn't just invent life and then watch from afar, way up in Heaven. Jesus came down to Earth to be born as a human being and to learn *exactly* what it means to live as a human.

Just consider these verses:

"Therefore, since we have a great high priest who has ascended into heaven, Jesus the Son of God, let us hold firmly to the faith we profess. **For we do not have a high priest who is unable to empathize with our weaknesses, but we have one who has been tempted in every way, just as we are**—*yet he did not sin. Let us then approach God's throne of grace with confidence, so that we may receive mercy and find grace to help us in our time of need."* – Hebrews 4:14-16

"He was despised and rejected by mankind, a man of suffering, and familiar with pain." – Isaiah 53:3b

"Because he himself suffered when he was tempted, he is able to help those who are being tempted." – Hebrews 2:18

No matter what you're going through today, Jesus has been through either the exact same thing or something very similar. He understands exactly what you're going through, and He knows how much it hurts.

- Have you ever been rejected by friends or family? So has Jesus. John 7:5 tells us, *"For even his own brothers did not believe in him."*

- Have you ever grieved the loss of a friend or loved one? So has Jesus. John 11:35 tells us *"Jesus wept"* after his friend Lazarus has died.

- Are you worried about your future, what it may hold and how you'll get through it? Jesus wasn't too excited about his future either *(and for good reason!)*. In Matthew 26:38, he tells his disciples, *"My soul is overwhelmed with sorrow to the point of death,"* referring to his upcoming death on the cross.

Verses like these remind us, no matter what you are going through today, you are not alone. God knows exactly how you feel. He's been there. He gets it. He understands. And He will absolutely see you through.

He has not forgotten about you, and you do not suffer in vain. Cling to His promises and you will see – the One who was faithful then **will** prove faithful again. Just you wait and see.

Chapter Nine: When God Says Wait

Have you ever been in a season of waiting? When you're ready to move ahead, but God says *"Not yet?"* And no matter how much you cry out, the answer doesn't change. Or perhaps you hear no answer at all. Just silence.

If trusting God through the tough seasons were the only burden we faced, that might not be so bad. The struggle is only intensified, however, when we are called into a season of waiting with no clear end in sight. Yes, we believe God will come through. But when? *How much longer, God, do we have to wait? And why?*

While it would be next to impossible for me to tell you with certainty why God is asking you to wait, there are four very common reasons it could be.

1. You're Not Ready

This situation happens in my house all. the. time. You see, I have a toddler who really likes to "help." And by help, I mean... she really isn't helpful at all. No matter how hard she tries, she typically creates **more** work for me when she tries to help.

Like when she sees me sweeping the floor, so she grabs the dustpan to help... and pushes all the dirt right out of the pile and right back all over the floor.

Or when she sees me folding laundry... and so she gathers up all the neatly folded and piled shirts and tosses them right back into the basket. Or she takes off with them and stuffs them in random drawers all throughout the house.

Moms of little ones, you know what I'm talking about!

It's not that she doesn't *want* to help. She truly does. It's adorable. But at just over a year old, she simply isn't old enough to help with all the grown-up tasks I need to have done in a day.

And sometimes that's just how it is with the tasks God needs to have done as well.

You *want* to help. You really do. You're excited! You're ready to go out into the world and make a difference! But you aren't **ready.**

And no matter *how* excited you are to begin the next phase of your life, God isn't likely to throw you in the deep end and let you drown. There's a time of preparation that must happen first. A time for you to gain the knowledge, skills and experience you need, and a time for you to grow in character and wisdom as well.

In fact, this is a pattern we see all throughout the Bible. When God places a great call on someone's life, He typically gives them a time of waiting and preparation as well. Even for Jesus himself!

• Jesus waited 18 years from his time in the temple until he began his public ministry at age 30. *(Luke 2:42, Luke 3:23)*

• Joseph waited about 13 years from the time he dreamed his prophetic dreams until he was called to interpret Pharaoh's dreams at age 30. *(Genesis 37:2, Genesis 41:46)*

• David waited several years from the time he was anointed future king until he actually became king at age 30. *(Historians disagree on the exact number). (1 Samuel 16:13, 2 Samuel 5:4)*

- Abraham waited 25 years from the time he received the Lord's promise (at age 75) until Sarah bore him a son at age 100. *(Genesis 12:4, Genesis 21:5)*

- Moses waited 80 years until the Lord called him to speak to Pharaoh. He waited through 10 plagues until Pharaoh finally relented. And then he and the Israelites spent 40 years wandering in the wilderness, waiting for God to bring them to the Promised Land. *(Exodus 7:7, Numbers 32:13)*

That's a long time to wait for goodness you've already been promised! But sometimes big plans call for lots of preparation, and God is faithful to give us the time that we will need.

2. You Still Have Sins and Baggage from Your Past

Alternately, perhaps the reason you aren't ready is because you're still clinging to past sins, hurts, or hang-ups, and God needs to free you from them before He can use you.

Think about it. Are there any sins in your life that you haven't yet been willing to get rid of? Are there any areas of your life where God has asked you to do something and you haven't yet obeyed? Do you still struggle with past hurts and hang-ups that God needs you to surrender and find freedom from first?

Sure, God doesn't expect us to be perfect before we can serve Him. We will always have things we struggle with. But God doesn't just let us sit in our sin and hurt. He cleans us, purifies us and prepares us for what He has in store next.

3. Others are Not Ready

It's also important to remember – we are not the only characters in the story God is working out in our lives. Even if *you* are ready for God's call on your life, other key players may not be.

• Are you waiting for God to fix your marriage? God may be waiting for your husband to soften his heart and obey.

• Are you waiting for God to heal your child? God may be waiting for just the right doctor to finish medical school or locate across the country so he can take care of your family.

• Are you waiting for a new job? God may be waiting for your future boss to trust Him enough to step out in faith and hire new employees.

Sure, God could force people to take action, but God is a patient God who gives people time to obey. In fact, Psalm 103:8 tells us, *"The Lord is compassionate and gracious, slow to anger, abounding in love."* He doesn't smite us when we don't listen the first time; He gives us a chance to come through. And that means sometimes we need to be patient and give Him a chance to come through as well.

Yes, it can be incredibly frustrating when you're on the waiting end of God's great plan, but aren't you so thankful for God's great love and patience when you're on the receiving end instead?

4. Circumstances are Not Ready

Similarly, it may simply not be time for God's ultimate plan to be put into place. After all, God doesn't always wait until right when He needs us to call us. Oftentimes, He starts preparing us and working on us in advance, which means there will be a time of waiting and anticipation.

This is similar to what we, as mothers, do when our children have a birthday or special occasion coming up. We don't wait until the day of the party to say, *"Surprise! We're having a party and all of your friends are already right outside!"* No, we start preparing our children and our homes in advance.

We talk about the big day and what it will be like. We plan what games we want to have at the party and who we want to come. We clean the house, clean our bodies, and buy new party clothes and decorations if we need to. We enjoy the day, but we also get a lot of enjoyment out of the anticipation and preparation as well.

And the same goes for God's plan for our lives. He doesn't show up out of nowhere and say *"Surprise! You're moving overseas to become a missionary today!"* or *"Surprise! Today is the day you're going to meet and marry your future husband!"* That'd be crazy.

Instead, He lets us know in advance so we can begin to get excited and get ready while we are still waiting on circumstances to fall into place.

When Waiting is Hard

It is important to note, however, that not all seasons of waiting look the same. While there is a chance you may receive your call early *(like Jesus did)*, there's also a chance that you may receive your call very late in life *(like Moses)*.

And while you may have a relatively peaceful period of waiting *(like Abraham did)*, there's also a chance you may face a very difficult season of waiting *(like Joseph or David)*.

When it comes to waiting, Joseph and David certainly did not have it easy. Joseph was harassed by his brothers, thrown into a well, sold into slavery and wrongly imprisoned for two years during his 13-year waiting period. David spent much of his hiding out in caves, running for his life, hunted by King Saul.

Just because you don't see God at work doesn't mean He isn't. And just because you're going through a tough season doesn't mean that you're on the wrong path. It simply means God is not finished with you yet.

How to Respond When God Says Wait

So now that you have some idea why God may be calling you to wait, what do you DO about it? How do you trust God through a season of waiting? Here are a few suggestions:

1. Pray

First, pray to make sure that the "wait" you hear is actually a "wait" and not just you being lazy. *(Hey, it happens!)*

Secondly, pray for more detail. What exactly does God want you to wait on? Is it just one opportunity that you need to hold off on, or do you need a more extensive period of rest where you opt out of all opportunities for the time being? Is there a specific reason you are being called to wait? Try to get a little extra clarification if you can.

2. Grow

Whether you are waiting because you aren't ready personally or because the timing simply isn't right yet, periods of waiting are a great time to grow and develop your faith so you are ready when the time is right. Spend this time wisely. Read your Bible, pray, rest, build your family, read a ton of Christian Living books, listen to Christian podcasts, practice putting God first – whatever you need to do to grow as a godly woman.

3. Stay Faithful

Walking in faith when you don't know what direction you are supposed to be heading isn't always easy. Thankfully, there are tons of Scripture verses we can use to help us stay motivated and faithful during tough times. Verses like these:

"but those who hope in the Lord will renew their strength. They will soar on wings like eagles; they will run and not grow weary, they will walk and not be faint." – Isaiah 40:31

"The Lord is good to those whose hope is in him, to the one who seeks him" – Lamentations 3:25

Just because you don't know the specifics of God's plan for you doesn't mean that now is a time to sit and do nothing. Continue growing and walking in faith so when God is ready for you, you'll be ready.

4. Discern

Waiting may feel torturous at times, but the good news is: it won't last forever. Eventually you will be called to action, and you'll have to be ready to figure out what your next steps should be. Unfortunately, next steps rarely come with a huge, blinking "Go this way!" light, however, so you'll need to do your best to discern which way you should go.

Spend some time in prayer and in the Word, but also make sure you connect with other godly friends whose advice you can trust. You may want that extra feedback when it comes time to discern which way God wants you to go next and if the seemingly great opportunities that will inevitably present themselves really are that great of opportunities after all.

I know. Whether you're waiting for a season of pain to end or a season of great purpose to begin, waiting is rarely fun. But it really is a gift that will serve you well going forward.

Be faithful during this time. Make the most of it. Rid your life of all the old baggage and equip yourself with all the knowledge and wisdom you can muster going forward.

Because someday your season of waiting will end, God will call you to something big and amazing and potentially terrifying, and you'll be glad you went through your season of waiting and hardship when you did.

Chapter Ten: Trusting God With Your Future Plans

Mary was still a young woman, likely between the ages of 12 and 16, when she heard the call of God for her life, and it wouldn't be an easy one. She would give birth to and raise the Savior of the World – God himself, in human form.

Can you even imagine what must have been going through her mind? Having a baby can be stressful enough, but knowing you are responsible for raising the Messiah – the long-awaited one who would someday bring about redemption and salvation for your entire race? Talk about a lot of responsibility!

Plus, what would her parents think? What would her friends think? What would her fiancée think? Would they believe Mary when she told them that she was called by God to mother the one her people had been waiting on for centuries? Would they believe her when she told them that she hadn't been unfaithful? Or would they call her crazy, or a liar, or worse?

Having a baby out of wedlock was a serious offense back then. Her entire life was about to change, through no fault of her own, and it certainly wasn't going to be easy.

And yet, look at Mary's response in Luke 1:38. She doesn't ask a lot of questions or demand all the details. She doesn't argue or try to persuade the Lord to do things her way instead. She doesn't say *"Maybe later, when I'm in a better place financially"* or *"Sure, I'll do that for you if you'll just do this one thing for me..."*

She simply says, *"I am the Lord's servant... May your word to me be fulfilled..."* Talk about faith!**Servanthood Throughout the Bible**

Servant... it's a simple word. And yet it means so much.

The Merriam-Webster Online Dictionary defines servant as *"one that serves others"* or *"one that performs duties about the person or home of a master or personal employer."*[3] Both of these definitions barely scratch the surface of what it means to be a servant in the Biblical sense, however.

In the Old Testament, the word "servant" is often used to refer to forced slaves, hired helpers and faithful attendants. For example, we read that Abraham had many servants in Genesis 30, that the Israelites were oppressed as Pharaoh's servants in Exodus 1, and that David considered himself the servant of the Lord in Psalm 116.

Under this definition of the word, a servant is basically someone who does the will of the one they work for. Servants don't make the decisions, give the orders or call the shots. They simply carry out their duties as they are instructed.

Servants and slaves were very common in Bible times *(though the Bible did set plenty of regulations for their protection and provision)*, so the term was one that would have been well-understood and familiar to the people of that time.

In the New Testament, however, the word "servant" takes on an additional meaning. Here, not only can the term "servant" refer to slaves, hired helpers and faithful attendants, but it can also refer to someone who lovingly and humbly puts the needs and well-being of others before his or her own.

We can see this in Mark 9:35, which reads, *"Sitting down, Jesus called the Twelve and said, 'Anyone who wants to be first must be the very last, and the **servant** of all'"* as well as in Mark 10:43-44, which reads, *"Not so with you. Instead, whoever wants to become great among you must be your **servant**, and whoever wants to be first must be **slave** of all."*

Did Jesus want his followers to become actual servants and slaves for each other? No, not at all. He simply wanted them to humble themselves and dedicate their lives in service of others, the same way Mark 10:45 tells us, *"For even the Son of Man did not come to be served, but to serve, and to give his life as a ransom for many."*

Both definitions of "servant" can be found throughout the Bible.

Mary: True Servanthood in Action

Going back to Mary's response to the angel, I believe Mary had some of both definitions in mind when she made her faith-filled response that day.

First, that she would submit herself to the Lord's leadership and direction, without trying to call the shots herself, just as a servant would submit her will and her plans to her master. And secondly, that she would humble herself enough to place the needs of others before her own, specifically the need of the world to have a savior before her desire to have a more comfortable life.

No, it wouldn't be easy. Following the Lord rarely is. But just as Mary faithfully laid her plans aside to put her full trust and confidence in the Lord's plans for her life, God expects us to do the same. To put aside our plans and our agenda, and submit ourselves in faith to His plan instead – no matter how scary that may seem at the time.

When God Asks Us to Do Scary Things

Mary may have been the only woman God asked to carry the Savior of the world, but she certainly wasn't the only Bible character God asked to do hard and scary things. Therefore, if God is asking you to do something big and scary for Him right now, you're certainly not alone.

For example:

• Noah was called to build an ark in the middle of a dessert and despite ridicule from those around him. *(Genesis 6:14)*

• Job endured great loss and suffering and still never turned his back on God. *(Job)*

• Esther risked her life to save her people. *(Esther 5, 7)*

• Daniel chose to honor and obey God even when it put his life in grave danger. *(Daniel 1:8)*

Can you even imagine how difficult it must have been to be in any of their shoes? No really. Stop and imagine it. I know you've heard the Bible stories countless times before, but can you imagine if **you** had to do any of those things?

What if God asked you to found a business or non-profit, to give up your dreams of ever having children or to become a missionary overseas? What if God asked you to give more generously than you felt you were able, to suffer through a chronic and painful illness for the rest of your life, or to bravely lead the fight for a cause you believe in?

Would you be courageous enough to confidently proclaim,

"Yes, God. I'm in!" Or would you shrink back in fear, unsure of your own abilities and hesitant to trust in God's provision for your life?

After all, it's one thing to trust that God can work miracles in others' lives. It's another to confidently believe He will work one in *yours*.

But remember – the Bible characters mentioned above didn't know how things would turn out either. They didn't see God's whole plan, and they had no way of knowing how everything would turn out. And yet, even without all of the details, they chose to trust God's plan anyway. Which is exactly what we are called to do as well.

Obedience Without Details

Honestly, one of the hardest parts of obeying God isn't doing the hard things themselves. It's the fact that we are called to trust and obey BEFORE we know all the details of the plan or how everything is going to work out.

Take the story of Abraham and Isaac for example. If you remember from earlier chapters, Abraham and his wife Sarah waited on God's promise to provide a son of their very own for **years**. First, they waited 75 years until they received the promise in the first place, and then another 25 years until the promise was fulfilled. That's a long time!

But then, as if that wasn't difficult enough, God asked Abraham to do something even harder: sacrifice his one and only son.

In Genesis 22:2, we read: *"Then God said, 'Take your son, your only son, whom you love—Isaac—and go to the region of*

Moriah. Sacrifice him there as a burnt offering on a mountain I will show you.'"

Can you even imagine? Honestly, I'm 100% sure my faith isn't strong enough for me to sacrifice my own son – not even close. But this is what God has asked Abraham to do after telling Abraham for years that He would give him this son as an inheritance.

And what does Abraham do? Does he question God to make sure he heard Him correctly? Flat out refuse? Try to negotiate a better option or say *"Surely there must be some other way?"*

No, we read in the very next verse: *"Early the next morning Abraham got up and loaded his donkey. He took with him two of his servants and his son Isaac. When he had cut enough wood for the burnt offering, he set out for the place God had told him about."*

Now, we do have some indication that Abraham didn't believe that God would actually require him to sacrifice his son. In verse five, Abraham tells his servants, *"We will worship and then we will come back to you,"* and in verse eight, Abraham tells his son *"God himself will provide the lamb for the burnt offering."* But still, he doesn't know for sure.

And yet, he doesn't waver or even procrastinate. Genesis 22:3 tells us Abraham got up **early** the next morning to load his donkey. I can't even manage to wake up early for things I want to do. I'm not ashamed to say I regularly hit the snooze button more than once and wait until my three-year-old comes in and jumps on the bed before I drag myself out from under the covers. And yet, Abraham doesn't procrastinate at all. He obeys, even when he doesn't know what God has planned.

And God isn't quick to let Abraham in on the plan, either. In fact, God lets Abraham go to the point where Abraham has physically bound Isaac and placed him on the altar and now has his knife in his hand, ready to slay his son, before God calls out to him to tell him to stop.

The Bible doesn't tell us how Abraham felt or responded emotionally during this scene. Was he fearful? Was he crying? Was he angry? We don't know. We just know that he obeyed, and that the Lord blessed him for it.

Now, I know how *I* would have obeyed in that situation. I wouldn't be on the mountain at all, much less with a knife in my hand. I'd be at home, wearing my cozy pants, snuggled up with my son on the couch, watching cartoons. I sure don't have that strong of faith, and I'm guessing you don't either. Abraham had way more faith than you or I likely ever will.

But how do you think Abraham got so much faith? Well, he had over 100 years of practice by this point! Through good times and bad, Abraham had spent the last 100 years trusting that God would come through. He had seen the Lord keep His promise by providing him with Isaac in the first place, and he was confident that the Lord could and would provide again. If God promised him a son, then he would have a son, even if Abraham didn't know how at the time.

Where There's a Will, There's a Way

As miraculous as Abraham's story is, Abraham isn't the only one God wants to do miracles through and for. God has something miraculous planned for your life as well. But it may not be easy.

You see, when we look at our difficulties, we have a tendency to view them through a human lens. We don't see a solution, so we assume there must not be one. We know God is calling us to more, but the world's answer is the only one that makes sense.

So what do we do? Well, we don't want to be rebellious, disobey God and miss out on His plans for our lives. But listening doesn't always seem like such a great option either. After all, God's plans sound too weird. Too scary. Too impossible.

So we try to negotiate. *"Surely You don't want me to do that,"* we think. *"Maybe I could just do this lesser thing instead..."* we offer. Or *"Sure... just as soon as I get in a better place financially...."* we reply.

We procrastinate. We try to find a way out of it. We try to find a better option. We tell ourselves that we're just making sure we heard correctly. We tell ourselves we're just being responsible. We have to take care of ourselves and our families.

But how many times is our procrastination simply a way to avoid obedience? We don't see the solution, we don't see the outcome, and we don't trust God. So we don't obey.

The good news is, however, that obedience really doesn't have to be as terrifying as it can sometimes sound, even if the situation looks bleak, hopeless or impossible at the time.

And that's because of 1 Corinthians 10:13, which reads, *"No temptation has overtaken you except what is common to mankind. And God is faithful; he will not let you be tempted beyond what you can bear. But when you are tempted, he will also provide a way out so that you can endure it."*

Let's break it down.

- *"No temptation has overtaken you except what is common to mankind"* – Are you tempted to do things your own way instead of faithfully following God? Yep, you're not alone. It's super common. It doesn't mean you're a bad Christian. It happens to all of us from time to time.

• *"And God is faithful"* – It doesn't say "if you obey, God will be faithful" or "if you're good enough, God will be faithful." Just "God is faithful." It's who He is. You can count on it.

• *"he will not let you be tempted beyond what you can bear"* – Worried God will give you more than you can handle? Don't be. He won't give you more than you can bear – with His help. *(See also: 2 Corinthians 1:8)*

• *"But when you are tempted"* – Not "if," but "when." We are all tempted by sin at some point.

• *"**he will also provide a way out** so that you can endure it"* – Yes! This right here is the key! No matter what you are going through today, if God is asking you to do hard things, God will also provide a way. He's God. He can do that!

When God Calls You to Big Things

So what is God calling you to today?

• Does God want you to stick it out in a tough marriage? *Then He will provide a way.*

• Is God asking you to give generously to those in need despite your low income? *Then He will provide a way.*

• Is God asking you to trust Him with your children and their future? *Then He will provide a way.*

- Is God asking you to serve others despite your current health issues? *Then He will provide a way.*

It doesn't matter what hard or scary thing God is calling you to do today. If it's in God's will, He will provide a way.

He may not provide it in advance. You may have to start walking in faith first and trust that He reveal Himself later. But, just because you don't know God's plan yet doesn't mean He doesn't have one. God will provide a way.

After all, God doesn't call you to do the impossible and then abandon you. He calls you to do your part and then trust Him with the rest.

And in the final section of this book, I'm going to show you how to do exactly that.

Section Three:

Living Out God's Plan for Your Life

Chapter Eleven: Trust Is a Choice

So up until this point in the book, I've given you a lot of knowledge. We've looked at four truths we can count on in tough times, why God allows us to go through tough times, and how God can use our past, present and future for His glory and our well-being, even if it doesn't seem like it at the time.

It's at this point, however, that we need to change directions.

Because even if I could give you all the knowledge in the world, it wouldn't be enough. It isn't enough to simply store Bible verses and Bible stories away in your head somewhere for future reference. You have to internalize them and apply them to your life for them to be useful.

It isn't enough to know *"God is trustworthy; He has a plan"* on paper. You have to live it out in real life too.

And before you can do that, you have to decide that you actually **want** to.

Your Faith, Your Choice

You see, just as God gives us free will when it comes to our day-to-day decisions, God also gives us free will when it comes to trusting Him. Faith is a gift, but it's only a gift for those who want it. God doesn't force it on us.

Instead, God provides us with just enough evidence that we can basically come to any conclusion we want. We can trust Him and see Him working in our lives if we want, but we don't have to if we'd rather not.

Lee Strobel gives an excellent illustration of this in his book, *The Case for Faith*. During his interview with philosopher Dallas Willard, the two have the following conversation:

"So," said Willard, "I asked the class, 'If this [miraculous event] really happened, how would Hanson respond?'"

I said, "You think he'd explain it away."

"Absolutely!" Willard replied. "It's very unfortunate, but I think he'd explain it away. We need to be alert to the fact that, in nearly every case imaginable, answered prayer can be explained away if you want to. And that's what people normally do. They say, 'Well, I'm very smart; I can't be fooled by all these things.'"

I could relate to that. I told Willard about the time when my newborn daughter was rushed into intensive care because of a mysterious illness that was threatening her life. The doctors weren't able to diagnose it. Even though I was an atheist, I was so desperate that I actually prayed and implored God—if he existed—to heal her. A short time later, she astounded everyone by suddenly getting completely better. The doctors were left scratching their heads.

"My response," I told Willard, "was to explain it away... I wouldn't even consider the possibility that God had acted. Instead, I stayed in my atheism.""

As unfortunate as it is, Strobel did exactly what many of us still do today. Even when Strobel was granted the incredible miracle he had just asked God to provide, he still ultimately chose to believe what he wanted to believe.

Is it any wonder then that God doesn't provide more miraculous signs? When those who already believe don't need them, and those who don't believe aren't likely to be persuaded anyway?

Honestly, it isn't the lack of miracles that's the problem. It's that people will always believe what they want to believe.

Consider for example, the most impressive series of miracles of all time: God himself is born in human flesh to a young virgin named Mary and is given the name Jesus. The baby Jesus grows up and performs an incredible number of miracles, including healing multiple people of life-long illnesses and raising three people from the dead. And not only that – but he even raises *himself* from the grave after three days and a very public crucifixion!

How much more of a miracle could you possibly need??

And yet look at what the Bible says in Matthew 28:17: *"When [the disciples] saw him, they worshiped him; **but some doubted**."* These aren't just random townspeople, either – these are Jesus's 11 closest disciples! If anyone had reason to trust and believe in Jesus, it was these guys! And yet, they still doubted.

And it's not like we can judge them for it. After all, how many times do we do the exact same thing?

God provides for us and provides miracles in all of our lives all the time. Way more often than we will ever realize or ever give Him credit for. And yet all too often, we simply explain them away as "good luck," as though God had no part in it at all.

And God allows this because He allows us free will. So those who actively seek God and His will for their lives find Him *(Matthew 7:7)*, while those who want nothing to do with God don't have to be bothered.

No, God won't force faith on us. Your level of faith is completely up to you.

Do You WANT to Get Well?

There's a verse in John that has always stuck out to me.

In chapter five, Jesus comes upon a man who had been an invalid for 38 years. Jesus does heal the man, but not before asking him one very peculiar question, which we read in verse six:

"When Jesus saw him lying there and learned that he had been in this condition for a long time, he asked him, 'Do you want to get well?'"

"Do you want to get well?" What a strange question. Of course the man would want to get well! He's been an invalid for 38 years! Why *wouldn't* he want to get well?

And yet, the more I reflect on this passage and read articles that others have written about it, the more it makes sense. Because how many times, if we were being completely honest, would we have to admit that truthfully, we're quite happy right where we are? Or at least happy enough to resist taking action to change.

For example,

- How many times have you made a New Year's Resolution to lose weight, only to grab for the cookies less than two weeks later? You say you want to lose weight, but do you *really*? More than you want to eat those cookies?

• You say you want to get out of debt and be in a better place financially, but do you *really*? Have you gone over your budget with a fine-tooth comb, looking for *any* extras you can cut out? Are you working around the clock to find a job, a second job, or even a third job to bring in that extra bit of cushion? Have you sold several of your belongings, even the ones you hold dear?

• You say you wish your marriage was better, but do you *really*? Have you read every single marriage book you can get your hands on, gone to marriage conferences, sought professional counseling, and braved your way through terribly uncomfortable, soul-bearing conversations with your husband, even though it's hard? Have you hit your knees in prayer more times than you can count and sought help and advice from godly friends? Or have you prioritized the comfort of letting things stay exactly the way they are over embracing God's will for you and your husband?

Yes, we all want to have great marriages and take care of our health and be set financially, but if we are truly being honest with ourselves, there are other things we want more. Yes, we want change, but not enough to do the work required. Staying where we are is hard, but changing is harder still. So we sit. We get complacent. We wish and we dream, but we don't *do*.

And it's the same with trusting God. We *say* we want to trust Him, but do we *really*?

Do we want it more than the comfort and security of staying right where we are and doing things the same way we've always done them? Enough to brave any obstacle and face any rejection that would come our way? Enough that we could care less what others think of us or what it might cost us to pursue a life radically sold out to God?

When we talk about wanting to trust God with our future, it isn't enough to say, *"Oh, that'd be nice..."* or even *"I really wish I had..."* You have to want it more than anything else in the world.

The Cost of Trusting God's Will

The problem with wanting a strong faith more than anything else in the world, however, is that in order to make our faith more of a priority, we must first push aside anything else that would threaten to take its place. This is the part of faith that no one likes to think about.

Sure, it's nice to dream about what great and amazing plans God might have for us in the future. It's great to think that He could use us to be a light in a dark world, to reach the lost, and to bring thousands of people back to Him. That He could use us to start huge ministries or even just to take care of the needs of those around us.

But have you ever considered at what cost?

Because, you should know, living a life dedicated to following God's plan isn't always easy. It comes with a cost, and sometimes that cost is high.

Luke 14:26 tells us, *"If anyone comes to me and does not hate father and mother, wife and children, brothers and sisters--yes, even their own life--such a person cannot be my disciple."*

Matthew 16:24-25 tells us, *"Then Jesus said to his disciples, "Whoever wants to be my disciple must deny themselves and take up their cross and follow me. For whoever wants to save their life will lose it, but whoever loses their life for me will find it."*

Does Jesus really expect us to hate our families and ourselves? Does he literally want us to carry around a huge, physical cross everywhere we go? No, of course not.

But he does require us to put him first above **all** else. Above our comfort. Above our own hopes and dreams for our future. Above the good we hope to accomplish someday. Above our goals and plans. Even above our own family, Jesus comes first. And everything else must be put down into its rightful place.

Choosing to walk in radical faith and trust of God's plan for your life won't be easy. It will require sacrifice, and there will be plenty of hardships. But one thing is for certain – it will be worth it.

Pick Up Your Mat and Walk

Continuing with the same Bible story as above *(Jesus healing the invalid man in John 5)*, look what happens in verses 8-9a, after the man replies to Jesus's question, *"Do you want to get well?"*

"Then Jesus said to him, "Get up! Pick up your mat and walk." At once the man was cured; he picked up his mat and walked."

Hallelujah, it's a miracle! The man is cured! But did you notice what happened next?

Jesus does his part, but he also asks the man to do his part as well. Jesus doesn't pick the man up and miraculously transport him where he wants to go. He doesn't move the man's legs for him, like a puppet.

No, Jesus gives the man the ability to walk, and then he tells the man to get up and do something about it. Jesus provides the healing, but the man must live it out if he wants to benefit from it.

Or consider Matthew 17:20b, in which Jesus says, *"...Truly I tell you, if you have faith as small as a mustard seed, you can say to this mountain, 'Move from here to there,' and it will move. Nothing will be impossible for you.'"*

How encouraging! If you have faith as small as a tiny little mustard seed *(which is a very small seed, by the way)*, **nothing** will be impossible for you! You can move a mountain!

But notice – the mountain doesn't jump up and move on its own, and God isn't physically coming down to pick it up for you. You have to actually step out in faith and *tell* the mountain to move, no matter how silly or pointless it feels or how ridiculous you think you look.

You can't just sit around waiting and hoping; you have to take action.

It's Time to Take Action

It's an incredibly crucial step, and yet, how often do we miss it altogether?

Sure, we pray without ceasing, but do we also get up and take action to help improve our situation? Or are we simply sitting around, waiting and hoping that God will miraculously fix everything for us and make everything just the way we like it, without us lifting a finger at all?

Are we being spiritually lazy, expecting God to do all the work for us? Or are we stepping out in faith to confidently take hold of all that God has promised us? Which do you think God will reward?

Just because our salvation is a free gift that we cannot earn does **not** mean that God expects us to sit around and do nothing at all until we reach Heaven. The term for this complacency is "lukewarm," and the Bible tells us exactly how God feels about lukewarm Christians in Revelations 3:15-16 *(and it isn't pretty)*:

"I know your deeds; you are neither cold nor hot. How I wish you were one or the other. So because you are lukewarm — neither hot nor cold — I am about to spit you out of My mouth!" Yikes!

No, the Bible makes it very clear that once we are Christians, we are expected to act like it. Just consider James 2:17 for example, which says *"In the same way, faith by itself, if it is not accompanied by action, is dead."*

It isn't enough to just believe; you have to act like. And that means not just praying *(which you absolutely should do)*, but taking radical action as well.

• If you are worried about the world your kids are going to grow up in, have you done something to change it? Do you volunteer in the inner-city schools? Have you written your congressperson? Have you opened your home and your family to a scared, pregnant teen with nowhere to go?

• If you are having marriage or family troubles, have you seen a counselor? Have you signed up for a marriage or family retreat? Can you truly say you've given it your all, or are you holding a piece of yourself and your heart back, waiting for the other person to put in the effort to earn it or deserve it?

• If you are struggling financially, have you started tithing faithfully, in accordance with Micah 3:10? Have you quit the job that was holding you back spiritually, trusting that God would provide another one in its place? Are you giving generously of both your time and your talents to those in need?

Yes, I know these actions don't make sense from a world perspective. We look at our relationships and our bank accounts and we say "I can't."

But the God we serve isn't limited to worldly manners of getting things done. Our God is a miracle worker.

That's why Jesus reminds us in Matthew 19:28b, "*...With man this is impossible, but **with God all things are possible.***"

Just because you don't see how God can possibly help your situation doesn't mean He can't. He absolutely can.

And the good news is, the more we trust God's plan, the easier it is to trust His plan and walk confidently in it going forward. The hard part is just getting started. And the next chapter is full of ideas for how to do just that.

Chapter Twelve: How to Trust God's Plan for Your Life

Okay, so you've decided you want to trust God's plan for your life. You believe that God is able to do all things, that He has your best interests at heart, and that He has a brilliant master plan He's busy working out behind the scenes. You are aware of the potential cost, but you don't care. You know God has something big in store, and you definitely want in.

So... now what? How do you step out in faith and trust God's plan, practically speaking? What does that look like? What do you actually *do?*

That's exactly what this chapter is going to address.

What Does Trusting God Look Like?

First, let's get clear on what trusting God does and does not look like, just so there is no confusion.

Trusting God's plan for your life does NOT mean:

• You have to give up all your biggest hopes and dreams and settle for a different calling you probably won't like very much.

• You have to trade in your job for a calling that is more "spiritual," like missionary, nun, or door-to-door evangelist.

• You have to be so super holy and spiritual that you never get to have any fun ever again.

• All your prayers will be answered, all your wishes will be fulfilled, and life will be easy peasy.

• You'll always know exactly what God wants you to do, what your next steps are or what His plan for you is.

• You'll always be confidently aware of His presence and how He is working in your life.

• You'll never experience any doubt, fear, anger, sadness or grief.

• Life is going to be a non-stop, super exciting roller coaster adventure from here on out.

Trusting God's Plan for your life DOES mean:

• You choose to believe that God knows best, even when you don't understand what He's up to.

• You commit to doing things God's way, even when it's hard *(and it will be at times)*.

• You continually seek God's will for every aspect of your life *(through prayer, Bible study and godly counsel)*, instead of simply making rash decisions on your own.

• You maintain an attitude of confident expectation and joyful anticipation, knowing that God **will** come through, even if you don't know how.

• You refuse to complain about your present circumstances and choose to look for the positive in every situation instead.

• You look for ways to honor and glorify God in every aspect of your life, even the ones that don't seem all that spiritual.

How to Trust God's Plan for Your Life

Okay, so if that's what trust looks like, how do we get there? How do we go from doubting God's goodness to walking confidently in the center of His will?

While there is no one exact blueprint, here are the steps I'd recommend to start.

1. Determine Where You are Placing Your Trust Right Now

We all place our trust somewhere. Where do you place yours? Do any of these thoughts sound familiar?

• If only we had more money... then I wouldn't be so stressed out.

• If my kids would just make better choices... then I wouldn't have to worry so much.

• If I could just get my spouse to act a certain way... then my life would be perfect.

• If I could just lose that last ten pounds... then I'd be able to look in the mirror without cringing.

• If only I didn't have this health condition to deal with... then I'd really be able to serve God like I want to.

- If only _____ … then I _____. *(You fill in the blank)*

Sure, having better behaved children, a more loving spouse and more money in the bank would be nice. But if you're placing your trust and your hope in your present circumstances, you're always going to be disappointed. There will always be new bills to pay, new health challenges to face and new arguments with loved ones to work through. Those things are never going away.

That's why, if you really want the peace that passes all understanding *(Philippians 4:7)*, you must learn to lean on the One who is greater than any circumstance we may face and who has all things under His control – God.

2. Bravely Bring to Light Any Obstacles that Prevent You from Trusting God

It's pretty difficult to make it through this life without acquiring at least a few hurts or hang-ups along the way. So, what are yours? Which situations or fears – past, current or future – are standing in your way from fully trusting God?

Chances are you probably have a few different ones – some you can name right away and others you'll have to prayerfully ask God to reveal to you.

Take out a sheet of paper and write them all down. Even the ones that are tough to face. Be brave enough to be honest with yourself and with God, and get it all out there in the open. No one has to see it but you.

For example, it could be:

- The untimely loss of a child or loved one.

- All the prayers that have gone unanswered.

- The struggles or hardships you've been through that you don't understand.

- The struggles or hardships you've witnessed others go through that you don't understand.

- The lingering doubts and questions that you're too scared to bring up.

- The lifestyle changes you'd have to make to fully embrace this Christianity thing.

- The poor example other "Christians" have set in the past.

- Fear of the unknown.

- What else?

There's nothing you can write down that God doesn't know already, and there's nothing you face that's too big for God. So just be honest with yourself. Get it down on paper and see it for what it truly is. It will help to know what you're really up against.

3. Pray for Stronger Faith

So, I know "pray about it" is a pretty stock answer in most Christian living circles, but there's a reason it's so widely recommended – it works!

Pray that God will heal your situation, but don't stop there. Pray that God will help you grow in faith and that you will have the strength and courage to follow Him wherever He leads.

Need an encouraging and relatable Bible passage? Check out Mark chapter 9, where we read the story of a boy who has been possessed by demons. The boy's father wants to trust Jesus to heal his son, but he's been let down in the past and doesn't know if he can.

Yet, consider the father's response to Jesus in verse 24: *"Immediately the boy's father exclaimed, 'I do believe; help me overcome my unbelief!'"* This is the same way we should respond to our doubts and struggles as well.

If you're struggling to trust God's Plan for your life, that's okay. God understands and He cares. Bring your doubts to Him in prayer and ask Him to help you trust Him more. He most certainly will.

4. Get to Know God

Of course, it's always going to be difficult to trust someone you don't know very well, so how well do you really know God? If the answer is *"Not as well as I should...,"* maybe that's something you need to work on.

The easiest way to get to know God better is simply to begin reading your Bible. After all, the Bible isn't just a dusty, old rule book. It's the dramatic story of God and His love for, faithfulness to and protection of His people throughout the ages.

The Gospels *(Matthew, Mark, Luke and John)* are a great place to learn more about what Jesus was like during his time here on Earth, while the Old Testament books *(particularly books like Genesis, Exodus, Esther, Daniel and Jonah)* are a great place to read about God and His relationship with His chosen people. Any of those would be a great place to start.

5. Learn God's Laws and Precepts

As we talked about in chapter nine, God doesn't just throw us into the deep end of our faith and expect us to obey Him with huge and scary things right away. Rather, He typically prepares us by asking us to follow Him faithfully in the little things first – things like obeying His laws and His commandments – before He calls us to embrace our main purpose in life.

So, are you following God in the little things? If not (or if you aren't sure), start there.

From Romans to Jude, the bulk of the books in the New Testament are letters written by early apostles and disciples to the various churches, teaching them how to live as Christians. These letters are practical, encouraging and powerful, and we still use them as our main source of guidance for proper Christian living today.

Another way to learn more about how to live like a Christian is to attend church regularly. Modern sermons are typically full of encouraging and instructional messages that can really help you learn how to live out your faith, whether you're brand new to Christianity or you've been around a long time.

6. Surround Yourself With Godly Influences

Church is also a great place to connect with other believers who can encourage you, strengthen you, and challenge you as you grow in faith.

There's a popular quote by motivational speaker Jim Rohn that says: *"You are the average of the five people you spend the most time with."*

While you won't find this exact number in the Bible, you will find plenty of verses that echo the same sentiment. Take Proverbs 13:20 for example, which says: *"Walk with the wise and become wise, for a companion of fools suffers harm."* Or 1 Corinthians 15:33, which says: *"Do not be misled: 'Bad company corrupts good character.'"* The truth is, the people you surround yourself with **will** have a tremendous impact on your faith so you must choose your friends and acquaintances wisely.

Take a minute to consider the five or so people you spend the most time with. Are they courageous, committed Christians who have dedicated themselves to radically following the Lord wherever He leads? Or are they lukewarm, or even negative, about Christianity and all that it entails? How has this affected your faith? *(Be honest!)*

If you're truly ready to step out in faith in a radical way, you really do need to make sure you have people in your life who are committed to doing the same.

7. Meditate on Scripture

Is there one particular worry or fear you find yourself struggling with more than any other? Look up applicable Scriptures, write them down, memorize them, and repeat them to yourself so often that they become a part of you.

Not sure which verses to meditate on? The Bible is full of encouraging verses on pretty much every topic imaginable – you just have to find a good one – and it's a lot easier than you might think.

Do a quick Google search for "Bible verses about ____" or just choose a good one from the list below:

"So do not fear, for I am with you;

do not be dismayed, for I am your God.

I will strengthen you and help you;

I will uphold you with my righteous right hand."

--Isaiah 41:10

"I keep my eyes always on the Lord.

With him at my right hand, I will not be shaken."

--Psalm 16:8

"For I know the plans I have for you," declares the Lord, "plans to prosper you and not to harm you, plans to give you hope and a future." – Jeremiah 29:11

"I can do all this through him who gives me strength." -- Philippians 4:13

Once you find a great verse, write it down, place it somewhere you'll see it often and repeat it to yourself again and again until you end up memorizing it. This way, it will always be at hand right when you need it.

8. Remember God's Faithfulness

When circumstances look grim, it can be so easy to forget all the ways God has been with us in the past. Counteract this by purposefully remembering all the blessings God has already provided you with. Make a list.

• What prayers has God answered?

• What blessings do you now have that you once hoped for?

• In what situations has God come through for you in the past?

• What fears did you once have that you no longer worry about?

Don't just write down the "big things." Take time to appreciate all the little things and the things you typically take for granted as well. Are you married? Do you have children, a home, a car, or a computer? Are there clothes in your closet and food in your fridge? Do you have the freedom to worship freely in the church of your choosing? Do you have friends and family you can always count on?

If so, God has already blessed you more than you know! He's done it before, and He'll do it again. Why would He quit now?

9. Look for Areas You Haven't Obeyed the Lord in the Past

Occasionally, I'll have a sweet lady email me at Equipping Godly Women, wondering why she never hears the Lord speak to her the way He does to others. And every time, without fail, I always ask the same question: *"Are there any areas of your life where you haven't obeyed something God has asked you to do or where you're currently living in sin?"*

For example:

• Is there anyone you need to forgive that you haven't fully forgiven yet or anyone you need to ask forgiveness from? *(If there's anyone you're regularly angry or annoyed with, that's a sign you haven't fully forgiven them.)*

• Are there any sins or bad habits that you refuse to let go of? *(Maybe gossip, pornography, gluttony or fear)*

• Are there any actions God has called you to do that you've refused to follow through on? *(Like tithing, having a difficult conversation with a loved one, or starting a new business)*

• Are there any dreams, hopes or plans God is calling you to lay aside – either for this season or forever? *(Perhaps a pregnancy, a career, a new home, or a certain relationship)*

- Are there any areas of your life where you're still trying to do things your way instead of God's way? *(This frequently involves inner tension, negotiations and even arguing with God.)*

You see, why would God ask you to do something new if you still haven't listened to what He has already asked you to do in the past? Why would God speak to you at all if you aren't going to listen?

Now, please understand, this is **not** always the case. Sometimes God is simply quiet because there isn't much to say right now and you just need to be patient. But it's definitely worth asking yourself, *"Are there any areas of my life where I've been disobedient or haven't listened and that I have yet to ask for forgiveness for?"* God may simply be patiently waiting for you, right where you saw Him last. It's worth considering.

10. Serve Others

Are you constantly consumed by worries and fears about your own life, your future or the future of your friends and family? If so, it may be time to turn your focus outward for a while, and serving others is a great way to do just that.

First Peter 4:10 tells us, *"Each of you should use whatever gift you have received to serve others, as faithful stewards of God's grace in its various forms."*

The good news is there are literally TONS of ways that you can serve other people with your time and talents. It doesn't matter how busy or how broke you are, you really don't have an excuse. You could:

- Donate the clothes and shoes your family has outgrown to a battered women and children's shelter.

- Play with puppies at the animal shelter.

- Volunteer at a local soup kitchen or homeless shelter.

- Train for and run in a charity 5K.

- Sponsor a needy child in a third-world country.

Someone out there is waiting on you to be an instrument of God's grace to them right when they need it most. Step out of your comfort zone to meet others at their time of greatest need, and you might just be surprised to see that God is right there with you too, meeting your greatest needs as well.

11. Practice Stepping Out in Faith

How do you learn to play basketball, ride a bike, tie your shoes or play the clarinet? You practice, practice, practice until you get good at it. And how do you learn to trust God and follow His will for your life? The same way – with lots of practice!

While it's easy to discount the small, seemingly insignificant things God is asking you to do every day, the truth is that these small steps of faith are incredibly important. Because it is with these little things that God teaches us, tests us and prepares us to be faithful in the big things He has in mind.

12. Accept that You Will Not Always Get Everything You Want

Okay, this is a hard one. But you can't skip it.

While I do believe that God will give us the desires of our heart when our hearts match up with His, this does not mean that all our wishes and requests will be answered the way we want or at the time we want.

In fact, there may very well be prayers you're praying right now that will *never* be answered or that will be answered in a way you don't like. And at some point, you must come to terms with that, as difficult as it may be.

Yes, you can grieve the dreams you'll never see fulfilled. You can get sad or angry or disappointed. God is a big God; He can take it. But ultimately you must lay down your own plans and expectations for your life so that you have the time and space to accommodate the amazing plans God has in store instead. Trust me, they're way better anyway, even if it doesn't feel like it at the time.

13. Do the Right Thing Even When It's Hard

Is trusting God always easy? Not in the slightest. I'm just going to be honest here.

In fact, did you know that according to a 2016 report by The Center for Studies on New Religions, Christianity is now the most persecuted religion worldwide?[4] Christians all across the globe are literally being tortured and murdered as we speak –

all because they are brave enough to claim Jesus's promises as their own. Wow.

While thankfully most of us here in the United States will likely never have to worry about torture or execution, that doesn't mean that trusting God's plan is always going to be easy. There will come times in all our lives when God calls us to do hard and scary things we honestly don't think we can do.

And it's during times like these when we simply have to take a deep breath, say a quick prayer, and move forward in faith and obedience anyway.

Is trusting God always easy? Not at all. But is it always worth it? Absolutely.

14. Seek Godly Counsel

Of course, being obedient to God's plan is a lot easier when you know exactly what God is calling you to do, but discerning God's will is a skill that can take time to develop. That's why, as you learn to listen to God's voice, it really helps to get the advice and opinion of other believers who can help confirm what it is you're hearing.

Proverbs 12:15 tells us, *"The way of fools seems right to them, but the wise listen to advice."* And don't stop at just one opinion, either. Proverbs 11:14 tells us, *"For lack of guidance a nation falls, but victory is won through many advisers."*

Every person has their own unique blind spots, stumbling points and ideas. Surround yourself with strong believers you can trust, and you're much more likely to get smart advice that will serve you well in life.

15. Commit to Following God's Truth Wherever It Takes You

And lastly, as you seek God's will for your life and do your best to confidently trust and follow Him in all things, you will eventually come to a point when God asks you to do something or believe something that you really don't want to. It may be sooner or later, but it's pretty much guaranteed.

Don't wait until that moment of hardship and struggle to decide if you want to follow God down that path. Decide now. Commit to following God's truth and God's will wherever He takes you. Even when you don't know what He's up to. Even when you don't agree. Even when it seems impossible.

God is God, and you are not. He's been around a lot longer than you have, He knows a lot more than you do, and He knows what He's doing. Just trust.

Chapter Thirteen: Dealing With Doubt

So now that you're armed with tons of knowledge, plenty of encouraging Bible verses and several very practical, actionable steps you can use to help you trust God's plan more starting today, you should be good to go, right? You can just wake up every morning, decide to trust God and follow His plan from here on out, and you're all set, right?

Unfortunately, it's not quite that simple. The unfortunate reality is that, no matter how much we want to trust God and follow Him closely, we all mess up and make mistakes at times. And even if your faith is rock-solid today, you could still falter and fail to trust tomorrow.

After all, isn't this the pattern we see all throughout the Bible? Even the most faithful and obedient Bible characters struggled with doubt, worry and fear at times.

Take these famous Bible characters for example:

• Abraham and Sarah both doubted that God would provide Sarah with a son, and even laughed when they heard the news. *(Genesis 17:15-17, 18:12)*

• Moses didn't believe God could use him to free the Israelites from Egyptian bondage, despite God showing him three separate miracles. *(Exodus 3-4:17)*

• Ten of the twelve spies doubted God would help them enter the Promised Land, even though He had just led them out of Egypt and had performed many amazing miracles along the way. *(Numbers 13)*

- Peter was smack dab in the middle of his own miracle – walking on water – when he began to doubt. *(Matthew 14:22-33)*

- Thomas refused to believe that Jesus was really risen from the dead until he touched the nail holes in Jesus's hands for himself. *(John 20:24-29)*

- John the Baptist questioned whether Jesus was really the long-awaited Messiah or if he should wait for someone else. *(Matthew 11:2-3)*

So if you have your own doubts, worries, questions or fears – whatever those may be – you're certainly not alone!

Faith: Assurance of What We Do Not See

The good news is, for every Bible story we have where someone doubts, we have many, many more Bible stories where God comes through, often in miraculous ways.

- God sent the ten plagues to free the Israelites from Egyptian oppression. *(Exodus 7-12)*

- God protected Shadrach, Meshach, and Abednego from being burned in the fiery furnace. *(Daniel 3)*

- God protected Daniel from being eaten in the lion's den. *(Daniel 6)*

- Jesus turned five loaves of bread and two fish into food for 5,000 hungry listeners. *(Matthew 14)*

- Jesus healed the woman who had suffered from an incurable bleeding disorder for twelve years. *(Luke 8:43-48)*

• Jesus raised Lazarus from the dead *(John 11:38-44)*

So why do we still doubt?

While there are plenty of reasons why we all doubt God's plan at times, one very common reason is that we simply do not have all the answers. We see the trials, but we don't see the purpose. We see the impossible situation, but we don't see the perfect solution God is already piecing together behind the scenes. We don't know what God is up to, so we wonder if He is up to anything at all.

And yet, when you look at the Biblical definition of faith, you find that knowing all the details isn't a prerequisite for faith at all. In fact, Hebrews 11:1 tells us: *"Now faith is confidence in what we hope for and* **assurance about what we do not see**.*"*

Faith doesn't mean that you know all the answers or that you know how everything is going to work out. It doesn't mean you never have fears, questions or doubts. It doesn't mean everything makes sense all the time. It doesn't mean you have God's plan all mapped out or even that you know what your next step is supposed to be.

No, God doesn't call us to know everything and approve of everything. That's His job. Our job is simply to follow where He leads and trust that He knows the way.

Evidence of What We Believe

There is one thing I want to point out, however. Just because God expects us to trust Him without all the answers does not mean that we are called to follow blindly, without any answers at all. Christianity is not a blind faith, and you do not have to abandon all common sense and reason to follow it. Not in the slightest.

In fact, God has provided us with literally TONS of evidence and scientific proof that provide credibility to the Christian faith. We simply have to seek it out.

And seek it out we should. A faith that is based on *"Well, my Sunday School teacher taught me..."* or *"Well, my pastor says..."* likely isn't much of a faith at all. What if they were wrong? *(Mine were.)* How will you answer critics when they start asking tough questions? What happens when you start to have doubts, as everyone does from time to time?

First Peter 3:15 tells us to *"...Always be prepared to give an answer to everyone who asks you to give the reason for the hope that you have..."* It isn't enough to just believe. You need to have solid reasons why you believe as well.

In fact, did you know that the Greek word for faith – "pistis" – comes from the Greek word "peitho," which means "persuaded?"[5] That's the kind of faith God calls us to – a faith based on knowledge, reason, trust and personal experience, not a faith based on a stubborn adherence to hearsay.

Ready to begin researching the evidence for Christianity yourself, but not sure where to start? Three books I love and would absolutely recommend include: *The Case for Christ* by Lee Strobel, *Keeping Your Kids on God's Side* by Natasha Crain and *Cold-Case Christianity* by J. Warner Wallace. If you haven't read at least one of these three already, pick one and read it next. They're fantastic.

Dealing With Doubt

Unfortunately, no matter how strong your faith is or how much knowledge you have in favor of God and Christianity, all of us struggle with doubt at some point or another. It's pretty much inevitable. The good news is, it doesn't have to be a bad thing.

Doubting is not sinful. It's what you do with those doubts that counts. Will you remain in a place of doubt and disbelief, hardening your heart to the gospel and growing further and further away from God with each passing day? Or will you use the natural, normal doubts you feel from time to time to encourage you to draw closer to God, find answers to your questions, and grow your faith stronger than ever before? The choice is up to you.

Are you going through a time of doubt lately? Here are three things you can do right now to use that doubt to develop a strong, confident faith in God's plan.

1. Embrace God's Compassion

First, it's important to realize that God is not angry with us when we doubt, but He treats us with compassion. The Bible even tells us in Jude 1:22 to *"Be merciful to those who doubt."*

And we can see examples of this all throughout the Bible. Consider, for example, how Jesus responds when Peter starts to sink in the water in Matthew 14, when the father doubts Jesus's ability to heal his son in Mark 9, and when Thomas needs to see proof of Jesus's resurrection in John 20.

Jesus doesn't get angry and discipline them. He simply asks them to trust him, and then he provides each of them with exactly what they need. And God still does the same for us today.

2. Cry Out to God

Have you read the Psalms lately? If not, you should! Psalm after Psalm records King David's very honest emotions as he cries out to God. From the depths of despair to the heights of victory, David experiences it all, and he is not shy in telling God all about it.

Consider Psalm 13:1-2, for example, which says:

"How long, Lord? Will you forget me forever?

How long will you hide your face from me?

How long must I wrestle with my thoughts

and day after day have sorrow in my heart?

How long will my enemy triumph over me?"

David wasn't the only one who took his feelings to the Lord, either. In fact, even Jesus himself cried out to God in his despair shortly before his death on the cross. We read about it in Matthew 27:46, which says, *"About three in the afternoon Jesus cried out in a loud voice, 'Eli, Eli, lema sabachthani?' (which means 'My God, my God, why have you forsaken me?')."*

No matter what you are going through today, bring it to God in prayer, telling Him how you really feel. God is a big God. He can handle your biggest emotions and toughest circumstances, even when it feels like you can't any longer.

3. Choose to Move Forward in Faith

As comforting as it is to know that God cares and has compassion for us when we go through times of doubt, doubt is not a place you want to dwell in for long. You really do need to use those times of doubt to spur you on to grow in faith, not just sit and wallow.

Need some motivation? Just consider what the Bible says about those without faith:

Hebrews 11:6 tells us, *"And **without faith it is impossible to please God**, because anyone who comes to him must believe that he exists and that he rewards those who earnestly seek him."*

James 1:6-8 tells us, *"But when you ask, you must believe and not doubt, because the one who doubts is like a wave of the sea, blown and tossed by the wind. That person should not expect to receive anything from the Lord. **Such a person is double-minded and unstable in all they do**."*

Yes, God will have compassion on you when you doubt, but He expects you to get up and keep walking in faith anyway.

Maybe you need to make a list of all the ways God has been faithful or of all the blessings He has given you in the past. Maybe you need to read your Bible more or pray without ceasing. Maybe you need to meet with godly friends who can encourage you and comfort you when you're down. Maybe you simply need to set your mind to walk in faith, even when you don't feel like it.

Whatever you need to do to continue to be obedient in whatever God has asked of you, just do it. Because God does have amazing plans in store for you, and they are all yours when you commit to walking confidently in the center of God's plan for your life, no matter how difficult it may seem at the time.

Conclusion

And now, we've made it to the end of this book. So, now what?

Well, you have the knowledge, you have the strategies, and you have the encouragement. And not only that... but if you're a believer, you even have the power of the Holy Spirit himself living right inside of you, empowering you to do great things.

In short, you have everything you need *right now* to go out and live a life of faith, fully confident in God and in His plan for your life.

So just one question remains – will you?

You see, it's a choice that only you can make, and it's a choice that you have to make every single day. Will you trust God's plan for your life, or will you put your trust in someone or something else?

• When your husband decides he'd rather hang out at the bar than go to church with you, how will you respond? Will you react with anger and fear? Or will you take your concerns to God in prayer, remembering that He loves your husband just as much as you do and that He still has a plan for his life, even if you can't see it at the time?

• When God asks you to give generously to a church, a non-profit organization or a family in need, how will you respond? Will you look at your bank account in worry, wondering how you'll make ends meet yourself? Or will you give generously, thanking God for using you as an instrument of His will for those in need, knowing that He is sure to provide for you as well?

• When someone you love is called back home to Heaven, how

will you respond? Will you react with anger towards God, for taking away someone who meant so much to you? Or will you thank God for allowing you to have that person in your life for the time you had them?

Unfortunately, just because you are a Christian walking in faith does not mean you are immune to the struggles of the world. In fact, John 16:33 tells us *"...In this world you will have trouble..."*

You will still have tough seasons. You will have hurts and heartbreaks. You will grieve over loss. God may never cure you or your loved ones, the hopes and dreams you have for your future may never come true, and the plans God has for you instead may not be what you expect.

No, you can't always control the tough situation you find yourself in, but you can control your response. So how will you respond today?

Will you hold on to hurt, worry, sin and fear? Or will you confidently place your trust in God, knowing that He is able to use even your toughest situation for good? The choice is yours.

List of Citations

1. Strobel, Lee. The Case for Faith: A Journalist Investigates the Toughest Objections to Christianity. Grand Rapids, MI: Zondervan.com, 2014. Print.

2. Gallup, Inc. "Percentage of Christians in U.S. Drifting Down, but Still High." Gallup.com. Gallup, Inc., 24 Dec. 2015. Web. 13 Mar. 2017.
(http://www.gallup.com/poll/187955/percentage-christians-drifting-down-high.aspx)

3. "Servant." Merriam-Webster. Merriam-Webster, n.d. Web. <https://www.merriam-webster.com/dictionary/servant>.

4. Prestigiacomo, Amanda. "Report: Christianity Most Persecuted Religion Worldwide." Daily Wire. The Daily Wire, 13 Jan. 2017. Web. 13 Mar. 2017.
(http://www.dailywire.com/news/12386/report-christianity-most-persecuted-religion-amanda-prestigiacomo)

5. "Wrestling with Doubt And Disbelief." Wrestling with Doubt And Disbelief. Focus on the Family, 30 July 2015. Web. 13 Mar. 2017.
(http://family.custhelp.com/app/answers/detail/a_id/26327/~/wrestling-with-doubt-and-disbelief)

Resources

Biblegateway.com. BibleGateway, n.d. Web. <https://www.biblegateway.com/>.

Bridges, Jerry. Trusting God: Even When Life Hurts. Colorado Springs, CO: NavPress, 2008. Print.

Evans, Rachel Held. "Esther and Vashti: The Real Story." Rachel Held Evans. Rachel Held Evans, 9 Jan. 2012. Web. <https://rachelheldevans.com/blog/esther-and-vashti>.

GotQuestions.org. Got Questions Ministries, n.d. Web. <https://www.gotquestions.org/>.

Keller, Timothy. Walking with God through Pain and Suffering. New York: Riverhead, 2015. Print.

Meyer, Joyce. Enjoying Where You Are on the Way to Where You Are Going: Learning How to Live a Joyful Spirit-led Life. New York: Faith Words, 2002. Print.

Strobel, Lee. The Case for Christ: A Journalist's Personal Investigation of the Evidence for Jesus. Grand Rapids, MI: Zondervan, Willow Creek Resources, 2016. Print.

Strobel, Lee. The Case for Faith: A Journalist Investigates the Toughest Objections to Christianity. Grand Rapids, MI: Zondervan.com, 2014. Print.

Thompson, Elizabeth Laing. When God Says "Wait": Navigating Life's Detours and Delays without Losing Your Faith, Your Friends, or Your Mind. N.p.: Shiloh Run, 2017. Print.

Additional Resources

Loved the book and ready for more? Here are a few additional resources from Equipping Godly Women you might enjoy:

[Free] Trusting God's Plan Video Series: You have the knowledge – are you ready to put it into action? The Trusting God's Plan Video Series has just the encouragement you need.

[Free] Ignite Your Faith Challenge: Ready to challenge yourself to remove all obstacles and really dive deeper into your faith? The Ignite Your Faith Challenge is a five-day email series designed to help you do just that!

Putting God First: You put God first on Sunday mornings—what about the rest of the week? "Putting God First" is a book full of very practical, actionable steps you can use to put God first in your real life – starting today.

Find all of these great resources and more in the Equipping Godly Women shop: http://equippinggodlywomen.com/shop

Made in the USA
Coppell, TX
11 January 2021